JUSTIN TRUD[EAU] COVID-19 BIOMETRIC VACCINE TOTALITARIAN AGENDA

Peter Tremblay

Foreword by Dr. John Chang

Agora Books

Agora Books™
Ottawa, Canada

Justin Trudeau & The COVID-19 Biometric Vaccine Totalitarian Agenda

Agora Books
P.O. Box 24191
300 Eagleson Road
Kanata, Ontario K2M 2C3

Agora Books is a self-publishing agency for authors that was launched by The Agora Cosmopolitan which is a registered not-for-profit corporation.

ISBN 978-1-77838-010-5

Printed in Canada

Contents

FOREWORD

WHEN I ATTENDED MEDICAL SCHOOL to become a doctor, I did so in order to serve patients, not to serve some sort of corporate agenda. The axiom of my profession is to "do no harm." That's my Hippocratic Oath.

Thanks to Justin Trudeau and all the other spineless politicians across Canada, we now live in a society in which health policy is determined by the desires of multi-billion-dollar pharmaceutical companies. Apparently, there's no need for governments to subject their vaccines to rigorous independent analysis. If big pharma says the vaccine that they produce is good and in the interest of consumers to use, then that must be the case. At least that's what I am being told.

Supposedly, I'm to now turn a blind eye to any data or medical trauma my patients experience that stands in the way of vaccine consumption. If the first dose of the COVID vaccine makes my patients very sick, give them a second dose; if they get even sicker, or, God forbid, die, let their families bury them. Whatever you say to the family, make-up a pre-existing medical condition if you have to, and don't blame the vaccine.

If any doctor or scientist presents data that COVID-19 vaccines are anything but completely safe, they shall be labelled as spreaders of misinformation. We can't have these doctors or scientists standing in the way of progress now, can we?

Gone are the days of politicians like Tommy Douglas, who stood up to the medical lobby and its desire to exploit our citizens for commercial profit. If you want to keep your job at this hospital, or any other job in the medical profession for that matter, then toe the party line.

Well, my fellow Canadians, my integrity is not for sale. I stand in solidarity with numerous other members of my profession whose integrity is also not for sale.

Make no mistake, our failure as a society to defend the need for independent review and rigorous debate about COVID-19 vaccines will embolden pharmaceutical companies to expect the same red-carpet treatment on any future product they devise for commercial profits, no matter what injuries, mayhem, and destruction those products cause. Is that the future we want for ourselves and our children? We are speeding ahead into a Brave New World.

Across the planet, there have been no excess of deaths this year. That is, the worldwide mortality is not abnormally high. This does not jibe with the official narrative of a "killer virus."

The mortality of COVID-19 is on par with the mortality rate of influenza. Medical authorities who have declared this, or who have otherwise questioned the "killer virus" narrative, have been censored and publicly smeared. At my hospital, it has been as quiet as it has ever been. This is not like any pandemic that I have ever seen. Why isn't my hospital flooded with patients like all these hospitals that I have seen on cable TV news? It's good to see theatre outside of Toronto's entertainment districts and the streets of Broadway.

The lockdowns and restrictions have arguably been the cause of more harm and deaths than the coronavirus itself. While many physicians, particularly in my home country of Canada, publicly support the official narrative, others have admitted to being fearful of professional reprisal for questioning it. A growing number of physicians in other countries, including the U.S., Belgium, and Germany, have expressed clear dissent and even outrage over the positions taken by their governments and international health organizations.

Dr. Roger Hodkinson, a senior Canadian pathologist and expert in virology, when addressing Edmonton, Alberta city officials during a Zoom call, said, "There is utterly unfounded public hysteria driven by the media and politicians. It's outrageous. This is the greatest hoax ever perpetrated on an unsuspecting public."

Echoing the words of other experts, he also stated that nothing could be done to stop the spread of the virus besides protecting older, more vulnerable people. Indeed, "focused protection" has been proposed independently worldwide as the best strategy to combat mortality from the virus. However, the YouTube video of the Zoom call was removed for violating official policy a few days after being posted.

I have seen physicians and researchers I respect, admire, and agree with, censored, lied about, and even deplatformed over opinions expressed that do not fit the official narrative. So-called "fact-checking" websites like *Snopes* are particularly guilty of misleading and blatantly lying to us. And yet, entire legal teams in Canada, the U.S., and most notably Germany have independently brought major class action lawsuits against those deemed to be responsible for the misinformation and measures being propagated regarding the "pandemic."

There are gaping holes in the official killer virus and vaccine salvation pandemic narratives. Reliance on the PCR test for case counting is near universal, despite Dr. Kari Mullis, Nobel Laureate in Chemistry and inventor of the test, stating many years ago that it is simply a tool, and cannot be used alone to diagnose disease.

"It allows you to take a very minuscule amount of anything and make it measurable and then talk about it in meetings and stuff like it IS important," says the creator of the PCR test. But why then are positive COVID-19 tests being counted as cases, regardless of symptom status? These factors alone can cause a vastly overinflated case count. The little research being done on repurposing known therapies is being suppressed or ignored by international health agencies and governments alike.

Consider, for example, Dr. Pierre Kory, Associate Professor of Medicine at St. Luke's Aurora Medical Center. When addressing a U.S. Senate committee, Dr. Kory implored the National Institutes of Health to consider conclusive data on the profound efficacy of ivermectin, a WHO "Essential Medicine," in preventing the transmission and progression of COVID-19 illness.

Dr. Kory expressed dismay at the near complete absence of guidance for preventative and early treatment options apart from vaccines, which he called "unconscionable." He emphasized how he was one of many who felt the same way. And hydroxychloroquine, another "Essential Medicine" of the WHO, has been used the world over as an effective treatment despite the discouragement of this and other so-called health organizations that issued contradictory statements concerning its efficacy and availability.

Ever wonder why we don't really speak of the other corona-viruses known to infect humans, such as the original SARS or the ubiquitous influenzas?

Why is there no SARS vaccine being used?

Why are flu vaccines still being pushed, despite independent research clearly proving their ineffectiveness?

These coronaviruses are here to stay, and often manifest sea-sonally. *COVID-19 should be treated in a similar fashion.*

What happened to the concept of herd immunity with respect to COVID-19?

What happened to building stronger immune systems via life-style and supplementation and protecting the elderly and infirm, as we would with other viruses?

A world-renowned and award-winning German microbiol-ogist and physician, Dr. Sucharit Bhakdi, co-author of the book *Corona: False Alarm* (a bestseller in Germany and currently a bestseller on *Amazon*), and author of over three hundred peer-re-viewed articles in the fields of immunology, virology, and related areas, described as *"utter nonsense"* the claim of Dr. Anthony Fauci that 75% of Americans would need to take the COVID-19 vaccine in order to achieve herd immunity.

"Someone who says this has not the slightest inkling of the basics of immunology," Dr. Bhakdi told Fox News. When asked whether the vaccine is necessary, he stated, "I think it's downright dangerous. And I warn you—if you go along these lines, you are going to go to your doom."

Despite this, and so much more, the political-industrial com-plex appears obsessed with getting a vaccine into everyone. *Why?* There are those of us who have observed that the vaccines are part of a much more sinister plan: a move to introduce substances and technology into the bodies of people in order to label them with a form of biometric identification, alter their physiology, cognition, behaviour, and even their state of consciousness. The substances may even track and record people's actions, locations, and more.

Note that this is above and beyond the deleterious side effects and potential "pathogenic priming" that can, and has, occurred with attempts at coronavirus vaccines in the past.

Dr. Christiane Northrup, one of many dissenting physicians and herself a celebrated OBGYN and outspoken women's health advocate and author, discusses this in an interview, excerpts of which are included in this book.

Human beings could be reduced to products or commodities, made more compliant, susceptible to behaviour modification, as well as physiological and genetic changes that may make us more susceptible to future infection and illness, especially with the addition of the effects of the radiation from 5G technologies that are being disseminated throughout the planet. Because of their nature, the changes to the human species would likely be permanent.

Is any of this possible? Scientifically speaking, all of it absolutely is. And as this book expounds on, the technology exists, the patents are obtained, and the motives have been established. Simply put, the very nature of what it means to be human—our very biological, psychological, and genetic makeup—is being threatened. Our personal liberties are at stake.

What can we do? Dr. Northrup mentions groups of people, "freedom pods," who are openly asking questions and dissenting against the official narrative. This is how we do it. Health car practitioners, because of their oaths, have an obligation to "do no harm." But also remember that harm may be perpetrated through inaction as well, for as John Stuart Mill said in 1867, "Bad men need nothing more to compass their ends, than that good men should look on and do nothing." Working behind the scenes may at first be more effective.

But turning a blind eye to the inconsistencies and outright contradictions between the official narrative and reality may doom us all. Learn about the reality. I am a trained physician and scientist who asks you to please keep an objective open mind and to exercise critical judgement concerning the direction in which we are being led. We must take a stand to protect each other, and thus, the species, against any threat that seeks to subvert and constrain our liberties for the nefarious purposes of manipulation, control, and population management.

Make no mistake about it, *we may be fighting for no less than our human free will.* The time is now to exert that free will, individually and collectively, so that we might not lose it. We need to rise up to question, and ultimately to join others and take up action against the insidious developments that currently permeate our lives, the manifestations of an evil totalitarian biometric agenda.

I wish you Godspeed my fellow human beings.

—John Chang, M.D., Ph.D.

PROLOGUE

C OVID-19 IS NOT A VIRUS, but instead a series of symptoms. These symptoms have been the product of biological intrusion designed to produce certain reactions in the body that appear to be a virus, but in reality they are not. Evidence of the role of genetic engineering in the manifestation of a "pandemic" has been well-documented in the book *COVID-19: The Genetically Engineered Coronavirus Pandemic.* Justin Trudeau and his confederates have played key roles in withholding critical information to Canadians on their healthcare decisions regarding the "pandemic." At the same time, there has been an effort to use the regulatory authority of the government to cajole and coerce Canadians into taking COVID-19 "vaccines."

The architects of COVID-19 sought to simulate a virus that could be used to create a desirable panic to then corral the masses into taking their gene therapy device wrongfully dubbed a vaccine. Dr. David Martin, Nobel Laureate, and Dr. Luc Montagnier, among other learned doctors and scientists, have documented these findings, but their research has been censored by those who seek to reduce humanity to mechanical beings of artificial intelligence.

Calling the COVID-19 jab a "vaccine" is just as legitimate as calling a piece of plastic made to look like an apple an actual fruit. Your brain might be fool you into eating a plastic apple, but your body certainly won't react in the same way.

A vaccine is, and has always been, an entirely natural product that enables your body to respond in a natural way to galvanize immunization.

The manufacturers of this new gene therapy device have produced a nice sounding story that their "vaccine" will protect you from the "coronavirus." The problem with this story is that the "coronavirus," in the way they have presented it, doesn't actually exist. The Trudeau government knows this and is in on the big business charade.

Coronaviruses naturally exist in the human body as part of our biological evolution in a similar way that bacteria exist, and which we are more commonly aware of. The first thing that big business interests have sought to do with their partners, including the Trudeau government, is to fool the public that a coronavirus is some new foreign threat to the human body.

The second thing they have sought to do is to then create a myth that they have isolated a virus called "COVID-19" in a lab to then be able to produce a "vaccine," when they also have not.

The third thing they have sought to do is to collude with one another to disguise any visual, statistical, or other ample data that points to their role in an elaborate mass psychological operation. The problem is that censorship has never been used in history to stop misinformation; instead, it has always been used to conceal the truth, and it's apparent that this so-called pandemic is no exception to this rule.

The story promulgated by the Trudeau government and their partners is of a vaccine that was created to stop the "coronavirus," or even "COVID-19." But this claim is no more legitimate than the idea of a vaccine having been created against bacteria.

The participation of the Trudeau government in the sophistry of the so-called vaccine is literally a page out Adolf Hitler's *Mein Kamp*, which documents the technique of the "Big Lie." The idea of the Big Lie was to support your agenda with a falsehood so big that no one would want to believe it could be anything but the truth. Indeed, thanks to Operation Paperclip, which welcomed Nazi scientists and other personnel in top behind-the-scene positions in the United States and other western countries like Canada, the practice of Nazi mass psychological manipulation and other experiments against human populations are alive and well today. They are playing out now in the so-called pandemic.

Thanks to the efforts of Patrick King in Alberta, as presented on the *Stew Peters Show*, we now know that the Trudeau government is aware that it is participating in a crypto-Nazi mass psych ops deception. In civil litigation, Mr. King took the public health authorities of the government of Alberta to court, demanding that they present evidence that the "SARS-COVID-19" virus had been isolated in a lab to prove its actual existence.

The judge allowed Mr. King to subpoena Deena Hinshaw, the chief medical officer of Alberta, to show proof of the laboratory isolation of "SARS-COVID" as an actual virus. In response, the chief medical officer admitted in court that she has no material evidence that the virus exists. (Appendix A-1) In response, the attorney general's representative of the Trudeau government sought to take over the case and was also unable to produce any evidence that the virus exists. In response, Deena Hinshaw's Office's said that "the science doesn't matter."

Mr. King refers to himself as "the most censored Canadian." Reportedly, Mr. King has not only been banned from social media like Facebook, he has even been banned from Google.

"COVID-19" is, thus, not a self-contained virus, but instead a series of symptoms, the by-product of a laboratory-concocted negative coronavirus reaction. Dr. Lee Merritt's research suggests that some kind of bioweapon has been spread through Earth's atmosphere to artificially induce COVID-19 symptoms among vulnerable populations. Think of this reaction like someone sneaking into your stomach a bad bowl of chili that had been sitting for days on a table at room temperature. The likely result would be food poisoning from all the harmful bacteria in your gut. Without knowing what was actually happening, you might be easily convinced you had a virus when you had actually experienced food poisoning or some other negative biological reaction. Well, it appears that's the kind of scam that governments, big business interests, and their partners are trying to play on everyone.

The "pandemic" has been a biogenetic attack against the most vulnerable people around the world, aimed at creating a cascading attack designed to mimic the appearance of a virus. The goal of this is to sell to the rest of the population that this is a virus in order to cajole and coerce them into accepting their gene therapy device as the only solution.

This biogenetic attack is the result of extensive research made into patents on how to weaponize natural coronavirus systems in the body to produce the symptoms that the WHO has sought to label as the "COVID-19 virus."

If the Trudeau government and their other partners were really concerned about your health, they wouldn't care if you took Vitamins C and D, ivermectin, or a host of other remedies people have already taken to recover from the Cabal's biogenetic attack without having to take their so-called vaccine. The Trudeau government would be simply thankful you got better, without caring about your chosen means to get better. But that's not the case. Trudeau and the Cabal doesn't want you to be able to freely examine any medical or scientific data other than the information approved by "experts" who have been endorsed by the same partnership which developed their highly profitable gene therapy device.

Doctors who went to medical school can see how big business lead by the World Health Organization (WHO) is trying to fool people with the collusion of governments like Trudeau's. These same doctors are being systematically censored and threatened with job termination if they don't support the Cabal's agenda. It is also notable that software developer Bill Gates is the biggest donor to the WHO, aside from the United States, so it is no wonder that the WHO has been coopted to seek to serve Bill Gates ambitions for humanity in relation to gene therapy to enable the assimilation of human genetic materials by Artificial Intelligence.

The numerous doctors who have chosen to speak up include Dr. Charles Hoffe in Canada and Dr. Peter McCullough, who have uncovered real information about the mad science behind the Cabal's AI gene therapy experiment against humanity. These whistleblowers have been viciously branded spreaders of misinformation. These doctors challenge the efforts of big business interests to literally sell-out humanity to their dystopia of altered human genetics. The testimony of Canadians doctors and others researchers have been cited in *YouTube, COVID-19 & The Cabal*.

Once you have some very basic medical training, it doesn't take rocket science to figure out that the so-called vaccine is actually gene therapy. Once one reads the published ingredients on the Health Canada website of the "vaccine," which appears to have intentionally failed to elaborate on what these formulations are, it is apparent that the ingredients are the components of a gene therapy device and don't meet the definition of an actual vaccine.

What everyone who takes the COVID gene therapy device is actually doing is giving an AI device and its programmers access to your body and its genetics through mRNA-nanotechnology software. This gene therapy device causes a variety of injuries and even death. This is the price people pay when they have volunteered their body to be part of an experiment; the experiment is to test the interfacing of artificial genetics with the complexity of different human bodies and natural genetics.

The effort of the Trudeau government to use federal powers to coerce Canadians into getting the COVID-19 gene therapy mechanism, which the Cabal dubs a vaccine, is therefore a grotesque violation of the *Canadian Charter of Rights and Freedoms* (Constitution Act, 1982) on multiple grounds. This includes Section 7, which specifically stipulates, "Everyone has the right to life, liberty and security of the person and the right not to be deprived thereof except in accordance with the principles of fundamental justice."

The Trudeau government also violates Section 2 (a) which protects the "freedom of conscience." This government has also sought to exploit the repression of free speech by big tech social media companies operating in Canada. The Trudeau government ought to have been chastising such violations of freedom of the press and other media of communication as guaranteed by Section 2 (b) of the Charter. Instead, the Trudeau government has conspired to subvert free speech during the "pandemic."

The Trudeau government, big tech, and the
COVID-19 gene therapy injections—aka "vacc
don't want you to hear or see any evidence th
"vaccine" is anything other than the greatest
bread. The book entitled *YouTube, COVID-19 e*
ments how doctors who dare cite any eviden
vaccine injuries in Canada are being subjected to punishment,
including firing for having been guilty of encouraging the new
"crime" of "vaccine hesitancy."

With that said, if we go to the Health Canada website, we can
see how the Trudeau government is hiding truth in plain sight
by listing the fancy names for vaccine ingredients without any
explanation of what they are and without any effort to inform
Canadians as to their documented health risks. If the Trudeau
government sought to act responsibly, then it would do.

Every generation witnesses horrific crimes against humanity, and this generation is no exception. In Canada, the crimes
against humanity committed against First Nations in relation
to residential schools show that governments in Canada are
also capable of executing crimes against humanity. The way in
which the Trudeau government has sought to add to crimes
against First Nations people by colluding in the cover-up of
the rape and murder of aboriginal women and continued other
atrocities against First Nations, visible minorities, and disenfranchised people who have been left to pick out of garbage cans for
food in cities like Toronto, or die in drug squalor in places like
Vancouver's East Side, testifies to the evil minds at work in the
Trudeau government.

The Trudeau government hypocritically ignores human
suffering in Canada alongside its efforts to financially support
the rich and the powerful, and the fact that the Trudeau gov-

nment has sought to support big pharmaceutical and biotech interests at the expense of Canadian lives should come as no surprise. With that said, our ability to spare future generations of such crimes against humanity relies on our ability to open our eyes to the evidence right before us.

The same Cabal group that was responsible for the residential schools is essentially the same clique that now backs the COVID-19 "vaccines." The only difference is that instead of selectively targeting First Nations, their targets are the whole population.

The use of so-called vaccines as weapons of mass destruction should not be a strange concept to people who are familiar with the histories of their use to "treat" the Spanish Flu in 1918. In Canada, First Nations are also familiar with how their women continue to be subjected to forced sterilization under the auspices of so-called experts, which the Trudeau government now wants us to rely on as the only source of good information about COVID-19.

It is notable that the COVID-19 "vaccine" interrupts women's periods, and can even "shed" onto women who haven't taken the vaccine, interrupting their periods as well. Dr. Lee Merritt confirms these reports. Notably, findings by Dr. Wolfgang Wodarg and Dr. Michael Yeadon published in *Undercurrents* suggests the COVID-19 vaccine could cause sterilization in 70% of the human population.

The negligence of the Trudeau government and its collaborators have all the necessary elements of violating Canadian criminal law regarding the COVID-19 "vaccine".

The first element of criminality relates to *Actus Reus*: a "wrongful deed," or guilty act. The Trudeau government has approved for use a product that has needlessly resulted in injuries and deaths, all of which could have been avoided if they did not approve for use a so-called vaccine for experimental use. When the Trudeau government forces Canadians to take a jab that is experimental, they are using illegal force to conscript Canadians to a corporate-pharmaceutical experiment that could result in permanent injury leading to death. The COVID-19 so-called vaccine has verifiably acted as a poison or toxic agent, and the Trudeau government bears criminal responsibility in its efforts to coerce Canadians to get the jab.

Pursuant to 245 (1) of the *Canadian Criminal Code*, "Every person who administers or causes to be administered to any other person or causes any other person to take poison or any other destructive or noxious thing is guilty."

The second element to establish whether a crime has been committed is *Mens Rea*: "a guilty mind," or the mental element. This is the Latin phrase for "The act will not make a person guilty unless the mind is also guilty." The axiomatic *Mens Rea* that the Trudeau government is responsible for is willful blindness, having ignored certain facts and information. The Trudeau government ignores the fact that COVID-19 is not an actual virus that a vaccine can treat. This fact is disregarded for the motive of enabling large transnational pharmaceutical and biotechnology companies based in Canada to work alongside other public-private partnerships to exploit billions of dollars in commercial profit at the expense of Canadian lives.

Furthermore, the Trudeau government has relied on data supplied by the very pharmaceutical manufacturers which stand to gain commercially from approval of their "vaccine." At the same time, Trudeau has ignored independent data from Canadian doctors and scientists who have sought to either pause or stop altogether the implementation of a so-called vaccine.

The third element of a crime can be efforts to collude in or exploit a pattern of concealment on the perpetration of a crime. In the case of the COVID-19 "vaccine," there is more than ample evidence of a collective effort to label, censor, and conceal as misinformation any and all evidence that the "vaccine" is not what the Trudeau government has alleged it to be

When law enforcement is attempting to solve a crime, a useful exercise is to try to go inside the head of the alleged criminal perpetrators. *If you were a computer software genius with financial interests in pharmaceutical companies and wanted to secure future commercial profits and thought of a plan to launch devices into human body, what would your goal be?* Would helping people build their immunities and lessen their dependency on pharmaceuticals help your commercial profit ambitions? *Not really.* By contrast, getting inside the human body to weaken immunity and increase dependency on your biotechnology formulations would definitely support your commercial profits. And, it appears that is what is going on with the COVID jab.

If you had concerns that there are just too many people on the planet, you might view getting your product labelled a "vaccine" as a "humane" solution that kills-off people while freeing-up resources for those people who do survive. It is apparent that these are the kind of minds at work in the effort to coerce people into taking the so-called vaccine, as corroborated by Dr. David Martin, Dr. Lee Merritt, Nobel Laureate Dr. Luc Montagnier—who discovered HIV—and numerous other doctors whose findings have been subjected to censorship by the Cabal and ignored by the Trudeau government.

Gibraltar has obtained an over 99% COVID-19 "vaccine" rate since June 1, 2021. Since that time, COVID-19 has soared to the point that in August 2021, the United States listed it as a country to avoid when travelling. Iceland, with over 70% of its population fully vaccinated, has also experienced a soar in COVID-19 symptoms.

Seychelles also has a high vaccine rate using the Astra-Zeneca "vaccine" approved in Canada. It too has experienced COVID-19 surges as a result of "variants" that are actually produced from the bodies of "vaccinated," and not as the result of people who are not-vaccinated. Indeed, it is apparent that the objective of forced vaccination is to subvert the body's natural biological defences' ability to be boosted from vitamins; this deficiency is the result of the introduction of the mRNA device and its artificial genetic manipulation.

Every time someone gets a "booster" shot, they will be receiving more artificial genetics injected into their body. This is a clear effort of the Cabal to transform humanity into a robot species with human sensory awareness that they can control. This is the kind of agenda that Dr. Miklos Lukacs de Pereny presents in the article titled, "Transhumanism: Expert exposes liberal billionaire elitists' 'Great Reset' agenda." This "transhumanism" agenda has been linked to a well-documented regressive alien agenda that has been elaborated by Dr. Michael Salla and by authors like Niger Kerner who wrote the book *Songs of the Greys*.

The Trudeau government's plans for a federal vaccine passport is no more virtuous than the motivations of an Opiod dealer on the streets of Vancouver. The Trudeau government doesn't give a damn about how many Canadians become injured, sick, or die as a result of being coerced into taking a jab. *Did you get blot clots because you had to take a jab to board a train going to Vancouver?* So what, in the view of the Trudeau government. *Did you get Bell's palsy because you're a single mother of three children working in the federal government and were coerced to take the jab?* Trudeau doesn't give a sh-t. *Did your spouse who was your household's only income earner die from the jab, leaving you with a life insurance policy that doesn't award money for vaccine deaths, which now leaves you on the verge of homelessness?* Trudeau also doesn't give a sh-t. Like any good Opiod dealer, Trudeau's only concern is about the commercial gain and power his government gains from the proceeds of a "drug." Veteran, critically acclaimed Canadian physicians are documenting the irrevocable damage that the pharmaceutical AI experiment on Canadian bodies is causing. But this is of no apparent concern to the Trudeau government and its partners who turn their backs against constitutional and criminal law.

In the *realpolitik* of the Trudeau government, why care about how coerced "vaccines" will affect ordinary Canadians when you have big donors with ties to pharmaceutical and bio-tech companies who all support the COVID "vaccine" agenda?

No one can accuse current Prime Minister Justin Trudeau of emulating his father's championing of rights and freedoms. Former Prime Minister Trudeau's passion for rights and freedoms propelled his efforts to repatriate the Canadian constitution from the United Kingdom alongside the creation of a *Canadian Charter of Rights and Freedoms* in 1982. Whereas Pierre Elliot Trudeau appreciated the affirmation of such rights in a democratic society, Justin Trudeau only appears to be concerned with doing what it takes to advance his political power without any regard to principle, ethics, truth, integrity, or the rule of law.

Justin Trudeau seems to blow in the direction of his biggest donors, irrespective of the best interests of Canadians. Whether his friends in the mainstream media and big tech collude to pull the wool over the eyes of Canadians into taking a jab which may not be in the best interests to their health is of no apparent concern to Trudeau. What matters to Trudeau is his role as Prime Minister of Canada is preserved, even if the pursuit of that power results in irrevocable harm to Canadians.

In the COVID-19 era of Canadian politics, Justin Trudeau shows us a governing class where leadership is in moral decay and operates at the behest of demonic shadows with financial power and with a political agenda diametrically opposed to the desires of civil Canadian society.

It is therefore apparent that the Justin Trudeau government and those politicians on Parliament Hill who support vaccine passports are not particularly concerned with keeping Canadians safe from COVID-19 because they know it's a scam. Rather, it is their desire to use vaccine passports to expedite a mass surveillance system in which the whereabouts of all Canadians will be tracked by "QR codes" linked to their smart phones.

Craig Kelly, a member of the Australian House of Representatives, shows us the direction in which Justin Trudeau and his confederates across political parties in the federal and provincial governments seek to take us. In Australia, thanks to the implementation of its QR code passport system, a veritable police state has developed in Melbourne, which only allows people to exercise just outside their homes for up to an hour, with travel up to a 5 KM radius in a perpetuated state of curfew.

Most people seem to think, for example, that multi-billionaire Amazon.com entrepreneur Jeff Bezos got rich as the result of selling books. But, that's not the case. Selling data is what catapulted Jeff Bezos and that 's what driving so-called "vaccine passports." "Passports" linked to everyone's smart phones will provide governments and big business alike a new frontier of commercial opportunity to use data to exploit and control people.

The mRNA ingredient in the unnatural biotech device is tan-tamount to a programmed piece of software that is injected into your body. Its architects allege that their "software" has been pro-grammed to trigger an immune response in your body. But there is a lack of independent clinical data over a period of many years to support such an assertion, other than the data they want you to see that has in turn been a product of redaction and censorship. But there is incontrovertible data to show that mRNA ingredient is actually part of a toxic stew that weakens the body and puts it under the control of artificial intelligence. This immediately available data is actively repressed by governments and big tech social media in the effort to force people to "vaccinate."

What Trudeau presents to Canadians as a "vaccine" is actually a toxic gene therapy device, and he seems determined to support the implanting of these devices into as many Canadians that he and other associates of the Cabal can coerce.

Aside from the mRNA device present in both the Health Canada approved Pfizer and Moderna jabs, take for example "ALC-0159 = 2-[(polyethylene glycol)-2000]-N,N-ditetra-decylacetamide" listed as a Pfizer ingredient on the Health Canada website. Most Canadians and other people would look at that long name and think nothing of it. But the U.S. National Library of Medicine documents this compound as "lipid nano-particle technology for therapeutic gene regulation." So, right on the Health Canada website, the evidence is in black and white that Canadians are being implanted with a biotech sponsored gene therapy and not a vaccine. Specifically, the U.S. National Library refers to this technology as a "gene editor" and as enabling "gene regulation" and potentially even "gene silencing" (Appendix A -2).

Health Canada acknowledges that the Astra-Zeneca product contains ChAdOx1-S [recombinant]. Research into this ingredient in well established scientific magazines and scholarly publications reveals that is a gene therapy enabling ingredient used to create a "Genetically Modified Organism." Anyone who takes this product being presented as a "vaccine" will also be subjected to molecular cloning. These scientific facts are not readily acknowledged by the Trudeau government on the Health Canada website. The website simply states that it was approved for use in Canada on February 26, 2021.

Polysorbate 80 is another notably harmful ingredient in the Astra-Zeneca and Janssen (Johnson & Johnson): Health Canada approved "vaccines" that have been linked to sterility, carcinogenic properties, and other terrible side effects. Pediatrician Lawrence Palevsky, MD, warns that Polysorbate 80 can enable the breakdown of the blood-brain barrier which will cause toxins from the human circulatory system to leach into the brain. The blood-brain barrier is particularly weak for children. This is particular troubling when it comes to Justin Trudeau's reckless push for the jabbing of kids who have an extremely low risk of contracting COVID-19 symptoms. Jabbing children with Polysorbate 80 and artificial biotechnology promises to create permanent damage in children, and in adults for that matter, that COVID-19 will not.

It is apparent that the Trudeau government and its partners could have saved lives during the "pandemic" if the goal were not to support a demonic big pharma agenda to conscript Canadian bodies for Artificial Intelligence inspired gene therapy experiments.

Magnesium chloride hexahydrate is also listed in the Astra-Zeneca "vaccine," and has also been linked to other side effects completely repressed by the Health Canada website because they don't want to educate Canadians in any way that would encourage "vaccine hesitancy." In other words, they want to advance the interests of big pharma and its partners. The side effects include depression, chronic fatigue, muscle cramps, and severe and ongoing diarrhea. Nps.org.au, which is funded by the Australian government, acknowledges other side effects ignored by Health Canada. These include flushing, nausea, vomiting, muscle weakness, blurred or double vision, loss of reflexes, breathing difficulties, irregular heartbeat, and a variety of other warnings for people who have certain medical conditions.

Health Canada and Public Health Ontario characterizes the "adenovirus vector vaccine," an active ingredient in both the Astra-Zeneca and Janssen (Johnson & Johnson) "vaccines" as "harmless." But America's venerated Mayo Clinic warns us otherwise. The listed side effects include difficulty in moving; fever; headaches; joint pain or swelling; muscle aches, cramping, pains, or stiffness; nausea; and unusual tiredness or weakness. Other potential side effects include anxiety; black, tarry stools; bleeding gums; blood in the urine or stool; blurred vision; chest pains; confusion; continuing ringing or buzzing or other unexplained noise in the ears; coughing; dizziness or lightheadedness; fainting; fast heartbeat; hearing loss; hives or welts, itching, skin rash; inability to move the arms and legs; numbness, weakness, or tingling in the arms or legs; pain, redness, or swelling in the arm or leg; pinpoint red spots on the skin; redness of the skin; seizures; stomach pain; trouble breathing; unusual bleeding or bruising; and vomiting blood. (Appendix A-3) Therefore, it is no wonder why so many people on Facebook and other social media have reported injuries and even death right after getting the jab.

WebMd.com links trisodium citrate dehydrate, another ingredient listed by the Janssen "vaccine," to nausea, vomiting, diarrhea, and stomach pain.

Overall, a report made by the Medical University of South Carolina acknowledges common side effects of the Janssen "vaccine's" mix of ingredients as including tiredness; headaches; muscle pain; chills; joint pain; fever; nausea; "feeling unwell"; swollen lymph nodes, along with a potential fast heartbeat, and a "rash all over the body."

Polyethylene glycol (PEG) 2000 DMG is one notable auxiliary ingredient in the Moderna jab. On WebMD.com, it has been linked with side effects that include irritation of the rectum; sleep disorders; excessive thirst; nausea; vomiting; stomach cramps; abdominal bloating; a feeling of general discomfort called malaise; intense abdominal pain and upper abdominal pain.

America's National Library of Medicine even graphically shows an example of how lipid nanoparticle technology infiltrates your body at the genetic level. (Appendix A-4) This NIH republished study also had support from the Canadian Institutes for Health Research (FDN 148469) and the NanoMedicines Innovation Network (NMIN), a Canadian Networks of Centres of Excellence (NCE) in nanomedicine.

Artificial nanotechnology is composed of nanoparticles that have been engineered into the COVD-19 gene therapy device. Thanks to nanomedicine that supports the design and research into mRNA gene therapy, scientists have now been able to configure what they officially call "brain machine interfaces," as documented by the Departments of Bioengineering and Neurosciences, Center for Engineered Natural Intelligence, and the University of California San Diego in the United States.

In "A New Frontier: The Convergence of Nanotechnology, Brain Machine Interfaces, and Artificial Intelligence," Gabriel A. Silva describes how the nanotechnology which Health Canada officially lists in its approved so-called "vaccine" is part of a new frontier of science designed to not only enable the editing, regulation, and silencing of your genes without your expressed permission, but also the mapping and potentially the control of even your brain function by a robot (Appendix A5).

After Canadian virologist Dr Byram Bridle linked the COVID-19 gene therapy mechanism to cardiovascular and brain damage, he went into hiding as a result of the combined efforts of disinformation agents under the Trudeau regime to prevent the truth from coming out.

In the United States, evidence of the plot is well documented on learned websites, but, in Canada, the Trudeau government has combined its efforts with provincial Colleges of Physicians and Surgeons that regulate doctors to silence those doctors who seek to present well documented evidence of injuries associated with COVID-19 gene therapy. It's therefore no wonder why Americans in general have been less gung-ho about taking the jab. Canadian public health authorities and the Canadian mainstream media have worked in tandem with the Trudeau government to deny information on what the "vaccine" really is.

In "What's Not Being Said About Pfizer Coronavirus Vaccine," Dr. Romeo Quijano, retired professor of Pharmacology and Toxicology at the College of Medicine, University of the Philippines Manila, noted some of the dangers of the experimental gene editing when applied to human vaccines. In this article, Quijano warns of "the danger that the vaccine might actually 'enhance' the pathogenicity of the virus, or make it more aggressive possibly due to antibody-dependent enhancement (ADE), as what happened with previous studies on test vaccines in animals, leading to a disastrous scenario."

If COVID-19 were genetically engineered, as documented in the book *COVID-19: The Genetically Engineered Coronavirus*

Pandemic, mutations or variants might be intentionally designed to provide biotech companies with a permanent "pandemic" state that can be exploited for more commercial profits and to help governments to justify more coercion against "the unvaccinated" as the misattributed source of "variants."

Notably, Bill Gates in 2018 presented in New York Council on Foreign Relations magazine, *Foreign Affairs*, a novel gene editing CRISPR technology that he had been effusively promoting as being able to "transform global development," and that his Gates Foundation had been financing gene editing developments for a vaccination program.

The Gates Foundation accounts for 45% of the World Health Organization's funding from nongovernmental entities, according to figures provided to Devex.com from the WHO. And, the only single-donor that has donated more money than Bill Gates has been the U.S. Government. It therefore doesn't take rocket science to figure out why the WHO has sought to rebrand the Gates Foundation's gene therapy technology concocted to re-design the human race as a "vaccine." This is corroborated by numerous sources, including doctors cited in *YouTube, COVID-19 & The Cabal*.

It is apparent that the Trudeau government, along with public health authorities on matters of COVID-19 gene therapy, are seeking to defend a Gates-sponsored project via the smokescreen that the WHO provides. Canadian doctors with years of professional experience and medical school training are being threatened and censored on behalf of the political-financial ambitions of a self-interested Cabal.

We may never find out the exact names of the people who were the actual criminal masterminds regarding the genetic engineering of COVID-19. But we must all shoulder the blame for putting up with an economic system in which the companies pursue insatiable profit. Under such a system, successful corporations are incentivized to be void of ethics. In such a milieu, if you're rich and powerful, why not engineer a biological weapon to scare people into taking a jab that you have created to redesign populations for you to control through artificial intelligence?

In a democracy, government ensures that an environment is fostered to enable citizens to make informed decisions. A democracy is also based upon respecting personal freedoms associated with enabling people to make choices over their own bodies.

The Trudeau government is coercing Canadians to take an experimental product that Health Canada has failed to properly educate Canadians about with regard to the nature of its ingredients. The applications for gene therapy involving nanotechnology and artificial intelligence is nothing short of a crime against humanity. The COVID-19 "vaccine" is a bioengineering application designed to genetically modify and control humans through the use of a third party artificial intelligence source. The COVID-19 "vaccine" does not seem to be the benign and non-invasive protector of human health from an alleged virus.

It is apparent that governments have authorized the use of a "vaccine" that they know could cause widespread injury and even death across population groups. That is apparently the case as governments, including those in Canada, have sought to protect the manufacturers of COVID-19 gene therapy from any and all liabilities. They are not working to protect public health as they purport to be. If they were, these governments would have enabled citizens to hold pharmaceutical and biotech companies accountable in court for any injuries and deaths through the litigation of science-based evidence linking their gene therapy tool to damage claims.

The Trudeau government is seeking to coerce Canadians to participate in a mass biotechnological experiment designed to enrich the manufacturers of a gene therapy, who have been raking in billions to enable their control of human bodies using the nanotechnology that they have designed for that purpose. By waiving any and all claims of liabilities, all partners in the production of the so-called vaccine have no financial incentive to ensure the safety of its product. Instead, they have successfully conscripted governments and marketing mouthpieces under the cover of authoritarian coordination by mainstream media and social media sharing sites as partners in crime.

It is also clear that Trudeau's "vaccine passport" agenda threatens to push Canada into becoming the kind of crypto-fascist police state society which now functions in Australia thanks to the implementation of its own QR code-based vaccine passport system. Australia shows us just how quickly thriving democracies are being transformed into replicas of an authoritarian society like that of the People's Republic of China. Justin Trudeau's biometric vaccine agenda is a world where Canadians are to be controlled by an artificial intelligence matrix that monitors and regulates all their movements in an effort to mitigate public health risks caused by the very nefarious activities of a Cabal.

Biometric passports will give "public-private" partnerships free reign to electronically store any personal characteristics about a person for whatever use such a partnership has in mind without the consent of individuals and in the name of national security protocols. When coupled with the data that biotech companies will be extracting from the gene therapy experiments, the "pandemic" presents a Cabal with unprecedented commercial profits and new opportunities to gather intelligence to support its political ambitions. Invariably, major donors will be grateful for the cooperation of the Trudeau regime in the Brave New World of biometric intelligence gathering that the "pandemic" has enabled.

For Canadians who don't aspire to being such major donors, it may be useful to come to grips with our collective experience of the "COVID-19 pandemic" as being part of an artificial time line. COVID-19 and the damage it causes is real, but the pandemic is not.

The pandemic is the product of an induced artificial state of consciousness in which the world you think you live in is the world that the Cabal wants you to live in. Its objective is anything but righteous, altruistic, and well-intentioned.

The pandemic is the manifestation of a well-planned control system that was revealed to the eyes of the public in a U.S. Government document entitled "Influenza Pandemic" presented by Jesse Ventura in his ground-breaking show, *Conspiracy Theory* (2010), in which he documented visual proof of deep conspiracies.

The illusion of a general pandemic is the result of a sophisticated orchestration by big business and government-owned mass-media, co-opted politicians, the misappropriation of mortality and other data as "COVID-19 cases." "Experts" and public health authorities are presenting a script designed to reflect the prejudices of the substantively Bill Gates-funded WHO, and corresponding efforts by social media like Twitter, Facebook, and YouTube to censor any visual and other proof of pandemic propaganda. That is the control system that the Trudeau governments and the other corrupted politicians on Parliament Hill, in provincial legislatures, and municipal governments, including Toronto, subscribe to.

The Trudeau government has failed miserably to educate and inform Canadians in their efforts to make personal healthcare choices during the so-called pandemic, and they have done so in association with other corrupted politicians and public health officials who have prostituted themselves to a hidden agenda.

PREFACE

IF YOU WERE WATCHING TELEVISION and a man on a show with a questionable reputation told you that he would ship you something to drink that would cure you of any ailment or disease, would you elect to blindly drink whatever he sent you in the mail? Would you then accuse someone who thought you should critically fact-check the ingredients in the solution you were contemplating to drink as some "conspiracy theorist" and drink the product anyway? *Of course not.* Having such blind faith would be a comfort to a fool. As a critically thinking and rational human being, you'd want to know what was in that product before you gulped it down.

Unfortunately, it is this kind of critical thinking that Big Business interests, who own the so-called mainstream media, along with social media giants like *Facebook*, has sought to deflect from any public debate. Having whipped-up the public into a state of fear about the psychopaths who genetically engineered COVID-19, as documented in my previous book entitled *COVID: The Genetically Engineered Pandemic*, this same mass media would now like you to blindly line up to get some vaccine product created by people you don't know with reported ties to a political-military-industrial complex that seeks to inject their substances into your veins without knowing anything about what they alleged will "protect you from COVID."

Pfizer, which has been a leader in the "race for a vaccine," has known ties to a political-military-industrial complex, and the pandemic reveals the ultimate agenda of this apparent self-serving and oppressive alliance.[12]

The alleged toxic ingredients of COVID-19 and other such vaccines include GMOs, mercury, and the following toxic agents.[3]

- acetone (solvent used in fingernail polish remover)
- ammonium sulfate
- amphotericin B
- betapropiolactone
- formalin
- gelatin
- glycerol
- hydrolized gelatin
- phenol red indicator
- phenoxyethanol (antifreeze)
- potassium diphosphate
- potassium monophosphate
- polymyxin B
- polysorbate 20
- polysorbate 80
- residual MRC5 proteins
- sorbitol
- streptomycin (antibiotic)
- tri(n)butylphosphate (neurotoxin)

Let's look at one such vaccine additive. According to the New Jersey Department of Health and Senior Services, "beta-Propiolactone is a CORROSIVE CHEMICAL, which can severely irritate and burn the eyes with possible permanent damage (corneal opacities)." Furthermore, they elaborate that "contact can irritate and burn the skin" and that "breathing beta-Propiolactone can irritate the nose, throat and lungs, causing coughing, wheezing and/or shortness of breath". They conclude that "Repeated or high exposure may affect the liver and kidneys."[4]

Polysorbate-80 has been linked to human sterility.[5]

Apropos to this book, bestselling author Dr. Christiane Northrup specifically reveals that the COVID-19 vaccine supported by Pfizer and other such Big Pharma interests have been laced with "biometric particles" designed to transmit data about you, including your sexual activities.[6]

Dr. Northrup reveals that the COVID-19 "mRNA (messenger *RNA*) vaccine" has been engineered through an MIT patent designed to resequence human DNA in support of an Artificial Intelligence (AI) inspired transhumanistic agenda.

When someone becomes "vaccinated," Dr. Northrup further reveals that they will constantly be acting as a transmitter of data about themselves to a global 5G network under the control of Big Brother ultra-insiders in Big Tech in tandem with a political-military-industrial complex. [Appendix]

In the *YouTube* interview in which she revealed this information, Dr. Christiane Northrup also revealed that she is a board-certified OBGYN physician, trained at Dartmouth Medical School, Tufts New England Medical Center. Dr. Northrup further elaborates that she is also a former Clinical Professor of OBGYN at the University of Vermont College of Medicine. She is the author of three *New York Times* best-selling books, including *Women's Bodies, Women's Wisdom, The Wisdom of Menopause,* and *Goddesses Never Age.*

Are such ingredients in a COVID-19 vaccine designed to promote immunity specifically or your health in general?

Lock and step with the proponents of a mass COVID-19 vaccination agenda are technocrats led by public health officials across Canada and all over the world, who will tell you to go buy a disposable facemask at your local store; never mind the fact that these masks are adding to the environmental plastic pollution in our cities and oceans. *If literally thousands upon thousands of medically trained doctors, registered nurses and other healthcare workers are catching COVID-19 with medical-grade facemasks, then how do you expect that your low-end store-bought facemask is going to protect you from someone around you who actually has COVID-19?* The real apparent agenda behind the facemask dictate is a mass psych ops, designed to use the pandemic to "acclimatize" populations to social control and a state of fear.

Every time you put on your facemask, the controllers want you to be reminded of the pandemic and whip you into a state of fear while not protecting you from COVID-19.

Do you ever notice that these public health officials never give out good information on how people can build up their immunity through a regimen of vitamin and mineral supplementation that people in China have successfully used to combat COVID-19? Instead, these officials preach about their near useless masks and "social distancing" all day in order to undermine communal activities and commerce and *"stay in your home until we can inject you with our vaccines."*

Every one of these public health officials parrots the same lines because their script comes from the ultra-insiders who orchestrated the pandemic in the first place with the aim of corralling you into lining-up every man, woman and child to be assimilated into their demonic scheme.

COVID-19 was hatched from a plan by ultra-insiders who are concerned about "overpopulation" and the challenge to their authority posed by human rights and environmental protection-inspired people and groups that oppose growing atrocities in the world. The solution to this problem in the view of the ultra-insiders would be to get everyone in the world to be injected with "substances," which would enable them to shorten life expectancies, cause sterility, track people and alter brain function in order to make them much more passive to authority.

It is apparent that COVID-19 was concocted to whip up mass hysteria to then point everyone to the "only" solution for their fear, which will be to get the vaccine as the only way to protect themselves and society from infection.

Incredible financial wealth among the world's multi-billionaires like Bill Gates, who have been allied with Big Business interests, has made them develop God-complexes in relationship to our planet Earth and humankind. Such billionaires have successfully infiltrated governments along with representative global health organizations under the pretext of "philanthropy" and "charity" when their ultimate agenda is far from charitable.

There are two big groups of people who like to pooh-pooh the idea of so-called "conspiracy theories". The first group is people in the masses who think that we live in a "global society" that is one big Sunday school, where everyone acts like they are members of the Boy Scouts and Girl Scouts. The other group is the ultra-insiders who perpetrate the conspiracies they don't want you to know about.

One of the most notorious and well-documented conspiracies in U.S. history was Operation Northwoods, which involved a U.S. intelligence plot to overthrow Fidel Castro's Cuban government. [7] With that said, perhaps one of the most famous conspiracies that led up to the Iraq War was the false claim that Saddam Hussein was stockpiling weapons of mass destruction.

There are four kinds of conspiracies. The first involves collaborations of people and groups that operate in a self-serving manner, generally for financial gain, but operate lawfully and with no interest in harming specific political/governmental interests or specific groups of people.

The second kind of conspiracy involves criminals working together or well-organized criminal organizations. The third kind involves third parties that operate as "terrorists" or criminals from the outside and seek to attack corporate or political/governmental interests.

The first three kinds of conspiracies tend to be monitored and caught by law enforcement if they begin to transgress criminal and other law.

It is apparent that the COVID-19 "plandemic" did not involve the first three kinds of conspiracies. Rather, the prevailing plandemic seems to involve a "conspiracy of the fourth kind."

That is to say; the COVID-19 plandemic was an apparent "high conspiracy" perpetrated by ultra-insiders, who are collectively far more powerful than even the Office of the President of the United States and comprises elements of the very ultra-insiders that President Trump has pledged to challenge during his presidency. That is why Trump and his close allies sought to "take a different approach" to the social control agenda pursued by those who seek to collaborate with the ultra-insiders who perpetrated the pandemic in the first place.

I refer to these ultra-insiders as the "archons" and document their ability to control law enforcement and a clique of judges alike in my book *Justin Trudeau, Judicial Corruption and the*

Supreme Court of Canada. They don't operate within the law but above it.

When U.S. President Donald Trump talked about his desire to "Drain the Swamp," he was referring to the ultra-insiders who have sought to control American and international politicians like puppets.[8]

This particular book paints a scenario of high corruption by ultra-insiders, who have the power to concoct and enforce a conspiracy as a result of their collective financial and political control in capitalism.

The research within this book is not the product of a so-called conspiracy "theory" but the result of careful analysis, observation, and direct experience of interests that thrive on mass deception as to their true agenda. Such ultra-insiders often love to hide behind "feel-good" causes like human rights, social justice, environmental protection, and vaccination programs but have no genuine intent.

The objective of such ultra-insiders is to associate with or completely embed themselves in these causes to ensure that if the public hears any allegation of their association with a conspiracy, the public will regard such allegations with total disbelief.

The deception at work is apparent upon hearing things like: "You mean Billy? *Naaah...* He is in charge of that big "help" for the people in the third-world organization. *He would never do anything like that.* Or you mean Jenny? *Naaah... She's a big environmentalist.* No way she would be working for the polluters and helping exploit children... That's nothing but a conspiracy theory!"

Deception in our world is becoming more apparent under the auspices of the ultra-insiders. There is a clear effort to have us believe, through the media, that "up is down" and "down is up."

This book explores the corresponding intrigue and machinations regarding COVID-19 vaccinations and further explores what is at stake — in Canada, in the U.S., and around the world.

Ultra-insiders have three essential desires in seeking to control your body. The first one is to inject you with toxic substances, as I described.

The mortality from these substances, which result in "untimely deaths," will be blamed on "pre-existing health conditions" or blamed on "unforeseen" mutations of COVID-19, which create more death and serve the depopulation agenda of ultra-insiders. Such a vaccination program has also been linked to infertility to further serve the ultra-insiders' focus on freeing-up global resources by getting rid of some people.

The second reported objective is to inject you with nanotechnology and a "biometric tattoo," which will enable you to be controlled and your movements tracked by AI.

The third corresponding objective is to assimilate you into essentially becoming a passive robot-like creature, which is the extension of a unified AI.

That will be accomplished by the apparent combination of GMOs, nanotechnology and DNA resequencing as a result of a "Molotov Cocktail" of toxic biochemical and biological reactions.

The "end-game" is reputed to be the future colonization of Earth by demonic alien groups that whistleblowers allege control global institutions in violation of human sovereignty that will use the remaining human populations as a slave species with no free will as a result of having been injected by COVID-19 so-called "vaccinations."

Sounds kooky, doesn't it? The Hon. Paul Hellyer is a former Canadian Minister of National Defence, who has talked voluminously about interactions between manipulative aliens and representative interests.[9] These are representative interests of the very ultra-insiders who sprung the prevailing plandemic against humanity. Having known and met The Hon. Paul Hellyer, I can tell you that he is as "straight as an arrow" as they come. If Mr. Hellyer says there are manipulative aliens consorting with ultra-insiders behind the back of their fellow humans, then that is the case. The scholars who will back The Hon. Paul Hellyer's representations include Dr. Michael Salla, along with independent researchers like David Icke, whistleblowers and contactees like Alex Collier, who describe hostile interactions with regressive aliens in alleged underground facilities, and numerous people who have become the victim on alien abductions, which included medical experiments.

Try asking the very political archons about these aliens, and you will either be ignored or they will try to change the subject on you rather than trying to outright deny their presence.

In my book entitled *Justin Trudeau, Judicial Corruption and the Supreme Court of Canada*, I include a graphical representation, courtesy of Dr. Michael Salla, which presents a myriad of manipulative alien groups, which have interacted with ultra-insiders over generations to produce conflicts ranging from religious extremism and terrorism to financial crises to outright wars.

COVID-19 is nothing short of an apparent plot to culminate all of these nefarious efforts in a pandemic-induced New World Order. The aim of this dystopian Order is to destroy rights and freedoms within human societies on our planet Earth in favour of a global totalitarian state in lockdown under the control of manipulative alien AI interests and psychopathic ultra-insiders with the pretext of the need to "protect public health and save lives." The real goal of the current elite sponsored efforts to drive our planet into a Hell of their own creation is to expedite the destruction of human lives and our planet Earth.

David Icke, who has documented the infiltration of ultra-insiders by manipulative extradimensional alien entities, has described the ultimate goal of the plandemic as being the "Hunger Games Society", when prevailing free economies that have also irrevocably crashed into a state of complete failure will be "re-set" into a "paperless economy."

Indeed, Dr. Northrop reveals the Bill Gates' patent WO/2020/060606 is designed to link everyone's biometric data into a cryptocurrency system controlled by ultra-insiders.[10]

Nikita Mikhalkov, the Oscar-winning Russian director, appearing on an episode of 'Besogan TV' was adamant that the patent is the unveiling of a *satanic plan to microchip the entire global population, and it was clear to him by the appearance of the devil's number "666" in the patent application*[11] *that* Satan is really a demonic alien entity. John Lash 's research into ancient Pagan Gnostics sought to warn humanity of AI as the incarnation of satanic aliens.

The ancient Pagan Gnostics sought to warn humanity long ago of the AI threat that now confronts humanity through the COVID-19 vaccine plot.

The "people" behind this plot may look like you and I, but as David Icke reveals, based upon this contact with indigenous tribal elders, they are not human at all.

Sounds funny, doesn't it? Ha-ha-ha! I can tell you this is no joke. I wish it was, though. I have met more than one of these entities. One of them who looked very human could, in fact, apparently read the mind of a human in much the same way as you can read a newspaper. And I don't mean just read "emotion" but read the exact words you are thinking.

If the ultra-insiders get their way, only people who have been microchipped from COVID-19 vaccines will be allowed to buy food and have a job through a biometric vaccine cryptocurrency system. Your cash, credit cards, along with your bank account, will be rendered useless.

People who refuse to be vaccinated in the "Brave New World" sought by the ultra-insiders will be sent to concentration camps under the pretext that they will pose a "public health risk" to the rest of society until they get vaccinated. As this book documents, this biometric vaccine experiment has already been well underway in Africa.

Dr. Christiane Northrup contends that over 99% of people will recover from COVID-19, but the effects that the vaccines will set off in human populations are without merit and irreversible.

The fight against the Biometric Vaccine Agenda is a fight for the very soul of what it means to be human against ultra-insiders who have risen to power in the shadow of various entities and their invasive AI technology. *Should we as humans be literally sold out by ultra-insiders to various entities through clandestine agreements that have apparently put us on the auction block? Or should we as humans begin to affirm our free will to be a sentient species, which embraces empathy, peace and love for each other and our environment? That is what's at stake.*

For all intents and purposes, COVID-19 is World War III by means of unconventional warfare. This means a World War launched against humanity, which doesn't involve clashing militaries or thermonuclear warfare but rather a virus launched by ultra-insiders under the cover of a mass-media system that they control. However, like World Wars I and II, the end-game of the belligerents is the same–the takeover of our planet under a global totalitarian state, where Big Brother controls a pacified population. And, like World Wars I and II, casualties have been high, communities destroyed, and the belligerents who this time seek to carry out their plan through microchipping under cover of "public health" are no less responsible for crimes against humanity.

References

1. *https://www.youtube.com/watch?v=MZZmSB8RPPc*
2. *https://www.militaryindustrialcomplex.com/totals.asp?this Contractor=Pfizer*
3. *https://thefreedomarticles.com/toxic-vaccine-adjuvants-the-top-10/*
4. *https://nj.gov/health/eoh/rtkweb/documents/fs/0228.pdf*
5. *https://www.cadth.ca/infertility-risk-hpv-vaccine-gardasil-containing-polysorbate-80-clinical-review-evidence*
6. *https://www.youtube.com/watch?v=UcGZC9P9WBg*
7. *https://en.wikipedia.org/wiki/Operation_Northwoods*
8. *https://www.dictionary.com/e/politics/drain-the-swamp/*
9. *https://www.dailymail.co.uk/video/news/video-1079464/Former-Defense-Minister-Aliens-live-us.html*
10. *https://patentscope.wipo.int/search/en/detail.jsf?docId= WO 2020060606&tab=PCTBIBLIO*
11. *https://blockchain.news/news/bill-gates-foundations-covid-19-vaccine-is-satanic-plot-says-oscar-winner*

INTRODUCTION

SOMETIME IN LATE 2019, THE world witnessed the emergence of a novel, severely contagious virus, later named the COVID-19 virus (also called the 2019-nCoV and SARS-CoV-2). Every scientist who has had a chance to examine the virus since its outbreak all came to the same conclusion–COVID-19 has properties that have never been seen before in any virus of its kind[1,2]. Of course this brought on a debate among intellectuals, as to whether this strange virus was indeed man-made or naturally occurring, with most of the evidence tilting towards the fact that the virus was manufactured in a Wuhan lab[3].

However, the world's governments do not seem to be completely unbiased on such a reasonable scientific inquiry. Instead, through the mainstream media, those who control governments appears to have sought to silence every scientist that has tried to tell the world about this bioengineered virus, labeling them conspiracy theorists. These powers that be, have also suppressed naturopathic treatments and methods like hydroxychloroquine in favour of a rush to push for a "vaccine" as the "cure-all" for COVID-19.

In the past, the topic of biometric vaccines and immunity passports have been brought up several times in many countries but have always been met with fierce resistance because the risks simply always outweighed the benefits. However, since the outbreak of the bioengineered virus, they have sprung a new narrative: "accept the vaccine or face death from the COVID-19 virus."

Faced with the fear of the COVID-19 virus, more people may just begin to consider accepting these vaccines. It is apparent that during a pandemic, many might be tempted to make a choice between protecting individual rights and confronting an existential threat to their right to health[4] and wouldn't this be convenient for Big Pharma?

The Gates Foundation has already committed $300 million to fighting the coronavirus and finding a vaccine. Tens of millions of that sum are dedicated to ensuring that vaccines are distributed in poor countries[5]. On the surface, the gestures may seem like charity, but what it really is, is an evil plot that could leave many of the world's most susceptible people at greater risk; it is also a plot to depopulate the world and to impose a totalitarian agenda on those whom the rich deem fit to remain alive.

In reality, the COVID-19 does not pose as much a threat to humanity as the mainstream media has painted. The COVID-19 mortality rates are greatly exaggerated to create fear and the biometric vaccines are still just as toxic as they've always been.

For Profit

E VER HEARD THE STORY OF one man who directed the bio-engineering of a lethal virus and then allowed this virus to be unleashed on humanity? The story is not fictitious, neither does it end here. The said man, under the pretext of protecting the world from this lethal virus, hatched a foolproof plan to impose a radical totalitarian agenda upon humanity.

The man in question is alleged to be Dr. Anthony Fauci, head of the National Institute for Allergy and Infectious Diseases (NIAID). In an exposé written by Dr. Peter R. Breggin, a Harvard-trained psychiatrist and former consultant at NIMH and his wife Ginger R. Breggin, Dr Fauci's COVID-19 treachery, his chilling ties to the Chinese military, and his entire role in the creation of the COVID-19 virus are brought to light.[6]

Breggin's exposé reveals how Fauci allegedly led one of the largest, most aggressive and most dangerous human interventions into nature in gain-of-function research in which a harmless virus was taken out of nature and engineered into a lethal pandemic pathogen. Fauci served as an extraordinarily destructive force in the world by sponsoring Chinese scientists to create SARS-CoV-2 and other deadly viruses for use as biological weapons.

Simultaneously, he developed chilling ties to the Chinese Communist Party and its military, financing their activities through NIAID and helping them to obtain valuable U.S. patents. Then, in collaboration with China and the WHO, he initially hid the origins and dangers of the pandemic, so that it spread more rapidly around the world. He then made himself out to be the messiah for the very pandemic that he helped to create, enormously increasing his power and influence, and the wealth of his institute and that of his global collaborators, including Bill Gates and the international pharmaceutical industry.

One of the greatest damages allegedly wreaked by Fauci in the course of the COVID-19 pandemic includes supporting the inflation of COVID-19 case counts and reported deaths from the CDC, then using the inflated estimates to justify oppressive public health measures that have no precedent and little or no scientific basis, but add to his influence and power and to the wealth of his globalist associates who just want to sell their hastily made vaccines.

Thanks to Fauci, most people are unaware of the truth about the 2019 coronavirus, which is the fact that only 6% of the so-called COVID-19 deaths have the virus listed as the sole cause of death. This means that in 94% of cases, patients had other underlying illnesses. Furthermore, most people who died due to COVID-19 were near or past their average longevity and also had other underlying illnesses. Having established these facts, Dr. Breggin argues that the risks associated with COVID-19 do not justify the drastic measures being imposed on humanity.

Peter R. Breggin, aside from being a leading reformer in psychiatry in the USA, is also a medical-legal expert, having unprecedented and unique knowledge about how the pharmaceutical industry too often commits fraud in researching and marketing drugs. He has testified several times in court in malpractice, product liability and criminal suits, mostly regarding adverse drug effects. He's also testified before federal agencies and the U.S. Congress, and he has been an expert on psychiatric drug adverse effects for the Federal Aviation Agency (FAA). He has also testified many times at FDA hearings.

Breggin's previous works have been cited innumerable times in worldwide media, such as *Time* magazine and *The New York Times*. He has also been featured countless times on reputable TV platforms such as *Oprah, 60 Minutes, 20/20, Larry King Live*, and *Good Morning America* to the *O'Reilly Factor* and Doug Kennedy on the *Fox News Channel*.[7]

Breggin's research alongside the research of several other reputable scientists have revealed that the virus was indeed created in a Chinese lab and intentionally inflicted on the world, all so that Dr. Fauci, backed by the likes of Bill Gates and the WHO, could further their cause of imposing a radical totalitarian agenda on humanity.

The Perfect Opportunity

THE FREE WILL AND PRIVACY of humans is presently being threatened by biometric vaccines which are apparently the hidden agenda of this pandemic. These biometric vaccines form the bedrock of a much larger plan of creating biometric identities for people all over the world. Big Business, alongside the State is colluding to create a society where your every move will be scrutinized. David Rockefeller, the late plutocrat and engineer of globalism had said at a United Nations dinner, "All we need is the right crisis and the people will accept the New World Order".[8]

The mainstream media has suppressed the flow of information to the public regarding COVID-19. People have essentially been jailed in their own homes as they observe strict lockdown measures put in place by the government. This has created panic and mass hysteria. An unprecedented crisis is unfolding right before our eyes, exactly what the United Nations has always wished for. Coronavirus has provided a perfect opportunity to push a totalitarian agenda of the New World Order.

A worldwide race for an effective vaccine has been triggered. The global elite and their technocrats will rake in high profits with this vaccine. But their ultimate agenda is much more sinister than that. The COVID-19 vaccine is being used as a platform for launching a worldwide Biometric Identification system. This is the perfect Trojan horse for the control seeking State to micromanage the life of ordinary people. It will emerge as a tool to weed out critics and adversaries by branding them as enemies of the State.

Skepticism regarding the COVID-19 vaccine is growing, and for good reasons. The State has a long history of misleading people. A glaring example of this was the 1976 Swine Flu breakout at a U.S. army base.[9] The State considered it to be a potential pandemic and President Gerald Ford authorized $135 million to develop a vaccine. About 25% of Americans were injected with the vaccine within 10 months but the global pandemic never came.[9] Instead the rushed vaccine resulted in injuries and unexplained illnesses in several people. The catastrophic response to COVID-19 has also demolished whatever little confidence people had in the State. History is about to repeat itself in the vaccine saga but this time it will have cataclysmic repercussions.

Biometric technology is already being used during the trial phases of the vaccine. A Boston based wearable tech firm, WHOOP, is developing a biometric smart band called the WHOOP Strap 3.0 in collaboration with G24 Healthcare.[9] This biometric band is to be used by volunteers in phase 3 of the trials. The WHOOP Strap 3.0 will collect biometric data from the volunteers like heart rate, respiratory rate, sleep performance and much more. Another company called SuperCom is helping governments to monitor quarantine and isolation. SuperCom provides a tracking biometric technology which includes a hypo-allergenic Bluetooth ankle bracelet, a smartphone and SAAS software in the cloud.[10] This system records the location of the patient whether in a building or a vehicle. The system is integrated with the smartphone and has secured communication, anti-tamper mechanism, fingerprint biometrics and voice communication. The aim is to use more permanent and less equipment driven biometric systems by the time the vaccine is rolled out.

Martin Armstrong, an American economic forecaster, is of the opinion that the State will covertly introduce a nanotech ID and a tracking chip along with a cocktail of vaccine toxins.[11] The plan is to somehow inject people with a biometric tracker. This can be achieved in a number of ways. Evidence of biometric nanotech is littered all over the place. The Bill and Melinda Gates Foundation and MIT, the Massachusetts Institute of Technology, have been working on similar technology. The prestigious *Scientific American* magazine reported on December 23rd, 2019 that a biometric tattoo had been developed by the collective efforts of MIT and the Bill and Melinda Gates Foundation.[12] This biometric tattoo can be used to inject a nanochip into the forearm while the person is being vaccinated. Bill Gates views this biometric tattoo as a "digital certificate" for an individual.[13] A special kind of ink is used for this tattoo and it is made using microneedles which do not leave any mark on the skin. It is essentially an invisible tattoo to track your every move. Your arm can be scanned to reveal your identity. Your vaccination, medical records and maybe some other confidential details too can be laid bare with a simple scan. This technology is burying the fundamental human right to privacy.

This biometric tattoo is part of a much bigger plan. In January 2020, a program called ID 2020 was announced at the World Economic Forum at Davos, Switzerland [14]. It was again sponsored by several billion dollar organizations including the Bill and Melinda Gates Foundation and the Rockefeller Foundation. The ID 2020 program seeks to create a digital ID for every person on the planet. It's using the false pretence of humanitarian grounds to further this agenda. The World Bank says that there are more than one billion people in the world without any ID [15] and it deprives them of the right to vote and other benefits. But an important thing to note is that the ID 2020 program while pretending to target such disenfranchised people, rather seeks to create a digital identity of every person for other purposes. Why do people who are already documented by the government still need digital ID?

According to *Off-Grid Healthcare* the objective of biometric IDs is to create a standardized data collection and retrieval format. [11] It will be used for cross-border sharing of identities of the entire population on the planet. There will be an AI-powered command center that will analyze the data collected by the biometric devices to calculate everyone's potential contribution and to identify threats to the system. It is a perfect tool for total surveillance of the people. This will end the concept of privacy as we know it. Your every single breath will be tracked and accounted for. It's a scary reality. The collusion between the State and the highly powerful private entities is making this program possible.

You may think that people will not allow such a draconian change in our lifestyle. But the mass media is already working on the mental conditioning of people. It is establishing that permanent changes to our way of living are inevitable. BBC News has already laid the grand vision of the society as intended by the technocrats as the "new normal". [16] The channel claimed that it will be a social reality by the year 2022. Ultimately people may not even have a choice in the matter. The State intends to make the COVID-19 vaccine mandatory for all. Those who resist the vaccine will be blacklisted and designated as public health criminals.

People who don't get a shot of this vaccine will essentially become social outcasts. They won't be able to avail many state facilities and even their civil liberties may be curtailed. This system sounds dangerously close to China's atrocious social credit system, under which people with low social credit cannot have a driver's license or apply for jobs.

Matt Hancock, UK's Secretary of State for Health and Social Care, recently suggested using a kind of "immunity certificate or a wristband".[17] This proposal sounds suspiciously similar to Bill Gates "digital certificate". Former Brexit secretary David Davis clearly admitted that the pandemic requires infringement of civil liberties. The UK did not have an ID card system since the two World Wars. But COVID-19 is being used to introduce biometric ID cards. This idea is deeply problematic. The phenomenon of biometric ID is not limited to the UK. A similar concept was also introduced in Kenya. India has collected one of the world's largest biometric databases in the form of Aadhaar cards. It records the fingerprints and the iris scans of people, which can be later used to reveal the complete identity of the individual. Aadhaar cards are being linked with everything, from bank accounts to tax records. This system puts people at the mercy of the government as all their confidential data is stored by the State. There have already been multiple breaches of the Aadhaar database in India, raising questions on the viability of such programs.

In the name of improving public health policy, VST Enterprises, a British cyber security firm, along with the government of the UK is planning to launch a COVI PASS [18]. It will be a Biometric RFID enabled Coronavirus Digital Health Passport. This pass will track and record all medical history of a person. A mobile phone can be used to biometrically access the information stored by the COVI PASS. RFID is Radio-Frequency Identification technology, with microchips embedded in tags which can be used to track the location of the carrier. Israel's Pangea, a company that provides digital transformation services, is also in the process of introducing biometric ID COVID-19 immunity passports as a means to enable countries to open their airports.[19] There will be a chip embedded in the card and it will be connected to the medical database of the country. A search engine will be able to access information gathered by the immunity passports and it will decide whether the card holder meets all requirements for entry into a country. If these types of immunity passports come into existence then travel will become impossible without sharing your life history with the government.

The game does not stop at a biometric vaccine; rather it is just the beginning. The ultimate goal is to create a society with biometric sensors at every nook and cranny. It is being claimed that fingerprint sensors are no longer safe because COVID-19 can spread through touch. Therefore more and more contactless biometrics will be introduced. Facial recognition technology has undergone tremendous improvement during the lockdown. Some companies are coming up with facial recognition software capable of verifying the identity of a person wearing a mask. China has already been aggressively rolling out facial recognition measures even before the pandemic. Use of facial recognition is justified on the basis that it will help to quickly regulate large crowds in confined spaces like airports.

But the wide use of biometric devices and gathering of data by the State raises a lot of privacy concerns. Such tools are viewed as measures adopted by authoritarian governments to quash dissent. Matt Gayford, the principal consultant at the Crypsis Group, warned that "Faced with a pandemic, the public may be rapidly accepting the risks involved with providing biometric data for healthcare services, but individuals should not be so quick to give up that data".[20] The misuse of this type of data collection has already surfaced in South Korea. The government used video surveillance, credit card tracking and phone location tracking to collect data of South Korean people. The update on these activities was shared by the government in the public domain. It led to widespread online harassment of people who were suspected to be COVID-19 carriers. The BBC reported a survey of 1000 South Koreans in which the researchers found that people were more afraid of the stigma associated with COVID-19 infection than the virus itself. [21] The *Moscow Times* reported that Russia is using facial recognition technology to enforce quarantine. A Chinese woman who travelled to Russia and failed to observe the two week quarantine was tracked down using this facial recognition technology.[20]

An app called 'StopCOVID' was launched in France but the Jean-Jaures Foundation reported that 53% of the French people will refuse to use the app due to privacy concerns.[21] In Poland too the government launched a biometric smartphone app to track people under the pretence of COVID-19. Facial recognition technology is also being increasingly used in America. Recently the American Civil Liberties Union (ACLU) filed a lawsuit against the Department of Homeland Security (DHS) over its use of facial recognition technology in airports; while California in September 2020 passed a bill to ban the use of facial recognition-equipped cameras by law enforcement.[20] Facial recognition technology can be combined with other measures including thermal imaging enhanced by AI, to better track citizens.[22] There are no specific guidelines for use of such technology and the data of citizens is being collected without their explicit consent.

The efforts of creating a biometric identity actually started in 2018, in preparation for the release of the COVID-19 virus. In July 2020 a public-private partnership program between the Bill Gates-backed GAVI, the Vaccine Alliance, Mastercard, and the AI identity authentication company Trust Stamp was ready to introduce a biometric identity platform in low-income remote communities in West Africa.[23] The program was first launched in late 2018 and it sought to create a "Wellness Pass," a digital vaccination record and identity system that is also linked to Mastercard's click-to-play system that is powered by its AI and machine learning technology. The Big Businesses have been using third-world countries as testing grounds for a biometric vaccine and the setting up of biometric identities.[24] Trust Stamp is trying to increase the commercial use of their contactless biometric technology. Their plans include the use of touchless identity verification for travel and insurance companies, customer screening for real estate agents, and parolee tracking without expensive ankle bracelets.[25] The COVID-19 pandemic provided a perfect opportunity to take this technology being tested in West Africa and use it all over the world.

China and the WHO claim that COVID-19 is a natural disease and a mutated strain of pre-existing coronavirus. However, one must consider the concerning reports that COVID-19 is actually man-made. China–the country where the virus was said to have originated–already has stringent control over its citizens. Reliable information rarely comes out of the country, so it is reasonable to conclude that they may not have been truthful about the origin of the virus. Dr. Li-Meng Yan, a Chinese virologist who managed to escape from China and is currently residing in the United States is one of the first Chinese whistleblowers to claim that COVID-19 was created in a laboratory in Wuhan.[22] Dr. Yan was requested to investigate the increasing number of pneumonia cases in Wuhan in December 2019. She believed that a highly mutated virus was in circulation. It later turned out to be COVID-19. But the Chinese State put pressure on her to remain silent. But she took the brave decision to make this information public and was forced to flee from China. Her social media accounts were suspended by the Chinese government. The WHO and China have collectively criticized and discredited Dr. Yan.

The revelation by Dr. Yan about COVID-19 is the missing piece of the story. It reveals the deep rooted agenda of the Bill & Melinda Gates Foundation, the WHO and Big Pharma to create a world that runs on biometric IDs. The timeline of the events makes it clear. The testing of biometric vaccines and biometric IDs disguised as the "Wellness Pass" was going on in West Africa since 2018. Bill Gates announced the biometric tattoo in December 2019. They needed an excuse to increase the use of biometrics all over the world. A mysterious man-made virus is exactly the way to achieve that goal. Facial recognition technology was improved during the lockdown and its use increased all over the world, including China, Russia, America and the UK. Once humans are implanted with a biometric device, like Bill Gates' proposed biometric tattoo, the State will control every aspect of day-to-day life. It is also suspected that implanting biometric devices might just be the start of the greater agenda of DNA alteration and creating a machine-based interface. Elon Musk has already discussed his plans to create a Neuralink.[26] He recently unveiled a pig named Gertrude with a coin sized chip in her brain. It was explained as a 'Fitbit in your skull'. Musk's ambition is to create superhuman cognition by using a brain-to-machine interface.

At the moment the world leaders are assuring people that the vaccine will be voluntary. But can one really trust them? If you refuse to take the biometric vaccine then you will be left out of the biometric ID program, unable to buy or sell anything including food.[24] That does not sound like the definition of voluntary. No politician is coming to save us and we must rely on ourselves.

PROBLEM-REACTION-SOLUTION

COVID-19 IS THE LATEST MANIFESTATION of the Problem-Reaction-Solution (PRS) strategy, says David Icke, former sports broadcaster and professional conspiracy theorist. Problem-Reaction-Solution is a mechanism used by the powerful, social ruling elite to manipulate and shape public opinion with the intention of gaining approval for the implementation of societal controls. Basically, with this approach, the government and other high powers in the society manipulate the population by introducing a problem to the society, eliciting a public reaction to this problem and then providing a solution. This virus has been unleashed upon the world–a manufactured problem that can invoke a reaction among the masses. In response to the public's call for action, the State will present the solution in the form of a vaccine. This is an ingenious ploy to force us into getting a vaccine that'll have disastrous impact on our freedom and privacy.

The planning to create the pandemic problem goes back to the 1990s, when the CDC and other organizations created several patents regarding coronavirus testing. David Icke explains that the entire world is basically controlled by a cult without states.

The ultimate goal of this cult is to create the "Hunger Games Society", a global world in which the richest and the elite, the tiny "one percent", controls the rest of the population.[27] This cult is also known as the Deep State. When the Deep State wants power which people will not freely give, it creates or exploits a problem by blaming it on others. Then the people react by asking the State for a solution and they are even willing to give up their rights in order to get that solution.

Terrorism is a classic example of this and now the 2019 coronavirus is also following the exact same pattern. The State then offers the solution which was already planned long before the crisis.[28] The 2019 coronavirus is a problem created by the so-called "one percent". This artificial problem is being used to instill fear among the masses. People have already begun asking for a solution to this manufactured pandemic and a vaccine is being championed as the magic cure. But this vaccine will be used to exercise complete control over people by depriving them of their freedom and privacy. The goal is to make people so scared and desperate that they will agree to this Draconian trade.

The PRS theory is also known as 'order out of chaos'. David Icke explains how the coronavirus is designed to push us into the era of technocracy. Currently, the fascist State is using all tools in its power to try to silence Icke and everyone else who dares to speak up on the massive propaganda currently going on. Icke's *YouTube* channel was deleted[29] and the video of his interview by *London Real* was banned by both *Facebook*[30] and *YouTube*.

The diagnosis of coronavirus is based upon certain symptoms and any person with those symptoms is diagnosed with coronavirus without looking into the possibility of another disease, many of which are also identified by the same symptoms. According to American doctors 80% of the people diagnosed with

COVID-19 have very mild symptoms [6]. This virus is dangerous only for elderly people with compromised immune systems or people suffering from preexisting conditions that have weakened their immune system. The logical solution would be to focus on protecting these people who are vulnerable to the virus. But the government chose to lock everyone up, even the people who are not at danger from the virus. This will have catastrophic effects upon the economy and that's exactly what they are trying to achieve with this pandemic.

The COVID-19 outbreak is not a random and sudden event as you've been led to believe by the mainstream media. Evidence shows years and years of planning was required to create the kind of scenarios we are facing today. In 2010, the Rockefeller Foundation published a document entitled "Scenarios for Future of Technology and International Development". This document discusses a scenario called 'Lock Step', in which a pandemic breaks out of China.[31] The Chinese government would use authoritarian measures to control the pandemic. The Western World would not use drastic measures right at the outset but would gradually introduce authoritarian regulations like China under the pretext of controlling the virus. Implementation of a global lockdown is also discussed in this document.

The present reality is eerily similar to the scenarios described in the Rockefeller Foundation document. Thereafter, in 2013, the former Governor of Minnesota Jesse Ventura uncovered the plans of the Centre for Disease Control and Prevention (CDC) to use a biological pandemic for invoking fear among the American public.[32] This pandemic would allow the government to impose martial law and to bring the military into the cities. Further investigation by Jesse Ventura revealed the existence of concentration camps in America. They were being called 'residential centers' and were designed to hold families. The plan was to create panic by using the pandemic and then lock people up in the so called 'residential centers' in the name of public health and controlling the virus.

Jesse Ventura also came across a very sinister agenda that year. The American government had set up 'fusion centers' which exist even today. These 'fusion centers' are used to fuse together all the data collected by various agencies in America like the FBI and CIA. Ventura interviewed former FBI Terrorism Specialist, Mike German, who revealed that these 'fusion centers' collect data which is not even related to criminality;[32] any information relating to 'extreme views' is also gathered and stored there. There is no oversight and regulation to define what constitutes 'extreme views'. This data is then used to apprehend people and groups that organize rallies for educating people about such places. Political dissidents are profiled and complete records are maintained on them. One big 'fusion center' is located in Colorado.

Hence, one can agree that the plan for creating a pandemic-like crisis obviously goes back decades. After much preparation the COVID-19 virus was unleashed upon the world. The New World Order has used China as a launching pad for spreading this virus. The Chinese authorities are furthering the agenda of the Deep State by claiming that COVID-19 is a natural virus. But that is not the truth. Dr. Li-Meng Yan, the aforementioned Chinese virologist, is the whistleblower who laid the pandemic plans bare. She discovered a highly mutated strain of a virus in December 2019 while investigating the rising number of pneumonia cases in Wuhan. The Chinese government exercises strict control over its people and doctors were told to keep the information of a new virus confidential. But Dr. Yan managed to escape China and is currently residing in America.

She claims that the COVID-19 virus is not natural and it has been created in a virology laboratory in Wuhan. According to Dr. Yan there is scientific evidence that proves that the coronavirus is man-made. The Chinese government has a patent of an experiment used to modify the genome of a virus. Viral genomes are like fingerprints and they can be examined to recognize the parts of the virus which are natural and which have been modified. The COVID-19 genome was examined by Dr. Yan and she concluded that 10% of the genome had been changed.[33] Coronavirus is like Frankenstein's monster–made in a lab from different parts to make it dangerous.

The original virus that originated from bats was not dangerous for humans but the modification made in the Wuhan lab has made the virus deadly for many people. There have been widespread efforts to silence Dr. Yan. The Chinese authorities · put pressure on Dr. Yan's family to bring her back to China. Fake Twitter and *Facebook* accounts created in Dr. Yan's name claimed that she had been kidnapped. She has been banned from Twitter while the fake accounts are still there. The WHO and other big corporations are combining their forces to discredit her. The authoritarian Chinese Communist Party runs a regime of fear and Dr. Yan is concerned that the West is also moving in that direction due to the fake propaganda. The Chinese government used testing kits with only 20-30% accuracy and that is how they manipulated data to mislead the public [33] Dr. Yan fears that COVID-19 may not have been the only man-made virus stored in the virology lab in Wuhan. She has urged the general public not to be misled by people with fancy titles.

David E. Martin, founder of IQ100 Index and a national intelligence analyst, says that the Center for Disease Control and Prevention (CDC) had actually patented coronavirus back

in 1999, when a strain of the virus had appeared in Asia.[27]
Creating a patent of natural processes and things is illegal
so the coronavirus could have been patented only if it was
made in a laboratory. The CDC also patented the kits used
for the detection of the coronavirus. Therefore the CDC had
the motive, means and a way to convert a biological virus into
profits. The research on the coronavirus continued in America
till 2014-2015 and then it was outsourced to a laboratory in
Wuhan in order to avoid blame and accuse China when the
pandemic struck.

In the Problem-Reaction-Solution method a strategic crisis
is placed on the existing political systems to accelerate drastic
global changes.[34] In light of all this evidence, it is clear how the
coronavirus is being used to change the way we live by destroying the world economic system. COVID-19 gave an excuse to
shut down the economy and force people into house arrest. The
lockdown will most severely affect small and medium businesses.
Almost all small and family run businesses manage to survive
on a daily income. These businesses do not have sound financial
backing like the big organizations. Forcing these small businesses
to close for a few months in the interest of public health is the
ideal ploy for destroying them.

Without daily income and no sound financial resources, the
small and medium businesses will die out and that is exactly the
goal behind this pandemic. The Deep State or the so-called "one
percent", want to create a society in which all means of production are controlled by big corporations. The plan is to use the
fear of a pandemic to create an enormous economic crash that
will kill the small businesses and clear the way for big corporations. Once the existing economic system is destroyed, a new
economic system tailor-made for the needs of big corporations

will take its place.[35] In the Hunger Games Society the control lies with massive organizations like Amazon.

The ultimate goal is to set up a one world government and to create a cashless society with one world currency. Even right now less and less businesses are accepting cash due to the fear of coronavirus. People are being misled into believing that they will catch the virus due to the germs and bacteria upon the currency notes. There is a big push to use cards and digital modes of payment.

Due to this virus millions of people across the world will lose their livelihood. They will have no choice but to depend on the government for survival. That is why discussions are going on to start a guaranteed universal income scheme. Desperate people will accept this income but it will be available only to those who abide by the rules and regulations of the New World Order.[35] The universal income is the perfect tool to exercise control.

The measures adopted by governments across the world to control the virus make no sense. All countries went into a lockdown which basically shut down the entire world. No one was able to come up with a different solution. This is nothing but economic suicide. People who are infected by the virus do not really die by the virus rather they die because their weak immune system is not able to cope with the virus. However no effort is being made to address this underlying problem.

The government should be using all the resources to boost the immune system of the elderly or people with preexisting health conditions. Instead all the focus is towards finding a vaccine when there might not be a need of any vaccine if all people have strong immunity.

Locking people in their homes has had no effect. According to government records the numbers of coronavirus cases are still on the rise.[36] So what is the justification for an ineffective lockdown? The government is only focused on finding a vaccine for COVID-19. This is because the vaccine is another way of exercising control on the public. The vaccine is the 'solution' given by the State but it is merely a front for achieving their agenda of taking away the freedom and privacy of the people. The vaccine will form the foundation of a biometric society with digital identities, where your every move will be tracked. People will be reduced to numbers and data.

Moreover, people may not have the freedom to deny taking the vaccine. The WHO, alongside several countries around the world is hinting that the coronavirus vaccine may be mandatory for all. Denmark has already passed a coronavirus related law that empowers the government to make the COVID-19 vaccine mandatory for all.[37]

This is a naked display of fascism, where the government decides what goes into the bodies of the people. People who refuse to take the vaccine will be vilified and demonized. They will become social outcasts and their rights will be curtailed. A system along the lines of the social credit system in China will be introduced for ensuring that everyone takes the vaccine. In China, millions of people are not allowed to board planes, trains or even apply for jobs when their social credit score falls below a certain level.[38] These mandatory vaccines will use biometric technology to keep medical records but it will essentially be a tracking device embedded in every human.

AI will dominate the new society. Most jobs will be taken up by AI and that will force an increasing number of people to the bottom of the Hunger Games Society. Potential threats and dissidents will be identified by AI-controlled command centers by analyzing the data collected by the biometric devices. There will be total surveillance and anyone who disagrees with the system will be apprehended immediately.[11] If this COVID-19 ploy succeeds then the future will be a bleak one. There is an attempt by the mainstream media to block information and only propagate the version of the WHO on COVID-19. At the present stage the goal is to create enough panic so that people will agree to take the vaccine. We must remain calm and push back against this biometric agenda to save our freedom and privacy.

Biometrics in Recent History

W E ARE ALREADY LIVING IN the era of computer vision and biometrics. But the Deep State plans to create a society completely dominated by biometric systems. COVID-19 is a tool for implanting biometrics inside humans. Biometrics can identify people based on their own biological or behavioral characteristics, instead of their associations, possessions or any secret information.[39] Need for a more accurate identification system was always advocated by the State for one reason or another, such as terrorism and now COVID-19.

Scientists have leveraged technology to expedite the process of human identification and authentication. Automated biometric systems have only become available over the last few decades, due to significant advances in the field of computer processing.[40] From printed IDs, we have come to the biometric ID, which lets you prove your identity without carrying any card or document. The use of biometric security can be seen everywhere including airports, public places, workplaces, offices and even on your smartphone. Biometric authentication is now commonplace.

The history of biometrics can be traced back to the 1800s when a system for identifying criminals called Bertillonage was developed by Alphonse Bertillon, an anthropologist.[41] Bertillonage was a form of anthropometry, a system by which measurements of the body are taken for classification and comparison purposes. But we are going to focus on the recent developments in biometrics that threaten our freedom and privacy. Sir Edward Henry, Inspector General of the Bengal Police, India, discovered the use of fingerprints as a method of identifying criminals in 1896. Soon the New York State Prisons started using fingerprints in 1903.[40] In 1969 the FBI pushed for automated fingerprint identification which required no human oversight and could produce quick results.[39] Over the years fingerprint identification has been perfected. Now identification by fingerprints has become so potent and readily available that almost every smartphone has a fingerprint sensor. Fingerprints are used as passwords for emails, bank accounts and other sensitive data. New and improved fingerprint sensors like the MULTICHECK-E are developed every day and they can be used to turn smartphones into complete biometric devices.[42]

In 1949, a British ophthalmologist J.H. Doggart noted, "Just as every human being has different fingerprints, so does the minute architecture of the iris exhibit variations in every subject examined. Its features represent a series of variable factors whose conceivable permutations and combinations are almost infinite."[39] This marked the beginning of human identification using iris patterns. Soon enough in the 1960s, the first semi-automatic face recognition system was developed by Woodrow W. Bledsoe under contract to the U.S. government. He developed a system using the RAND Tablet that could manually classify photos of faces.

Facial recognition moved towards more automation in the 1970s and finally in 1988 the first semi-automated facial recognition system was deployed. The turning point came in 1991 when real-time face recognition became possible. The result of this discovery meant that reliable real-time automated face recognition was possible.[40] In response to the events of September 11, 2001 the National Biometric Security Project (NBSP) was founded to accelerate development and deployment of biometric technologies. After the September 11, 2001 attacks, people felt that civil liberties were drastically affected by the incident. Common citizens had to go through thorough security checks and public surveillance with biometrics intensified. Europe also joined the biometrics race and the European Commission established the European Biometrics Forum.

The use of biometrics in U.S. security increased over the years. In 2004 the U.S. Department of Defense deployed the Automated Biometric Identification System (ABIS).[39] The primary objective of AIBS is to ensure national security from internal as well as external threats by analyzing biometric data. The regulations for these systems are very secretive and vague. 'Internal threat' can even mean a person who disagrees with and shows dissent towards the policies of the government. ABIS can perform biometric operations on fingerprints as well as facial images, voice samples, iris patterns, and even DNA. In 2006 the U.S. government organized an event called the Face Recognition Grand Challenge with the objective to promote and advance facial recognition technology designed to support existing facial recognition efforts.

Facial recognition is now used everywhere. In countries like China facial recognition technology is being used to exercise control over the people and identify political dissidents. As of now there are over 626 million facial recognition cameras in China.[43] By 2013 efforts began to make biometrics a part of mobile phones. Everyone is dependent on phones and turning phones into biometric devices has proved to be a masterstroke for gathering the public data. Big corporations like Amazon basically use this data to stalk you and manipulate your decisions.[44]

During the 2010s machine learning and AI were hard at work to make technology-based systems including biometrics smarter. Biometric systems had started using cutting edge machine learning and big data technologies to improve security as well as system performance. User Behavior Analytics (UBA), an approach based on user behavior uses Big Data and advanced algorithms to assess user risk.[39]

In recent years the use of multimodal biometrics which combines several biometric sources to improve security and accuracy has increased.[45] Several countries have started issuing biometric ID cards to their people and these cards also use multimodal biometrics. These IDs serve as a tool for identity verification using biometrics like fingerprints and iris patterns. India's biometric identity scheme, called the Aadhaar Card, holds biometric data of more than 1.2 billion people as of 2018. Biometric data include fingerprints, iris patterns and facial geometry of Indian citizens. Since its implementation, Aadhaar has been criticized for lack of proper data protection measures and several incidents of data leak.[39] These kinds of databases give power to the government over the citizens.

Biometrics, once limited to only a few applications and high-end facilities, is now everywhere. It carried the stigma of being a criminal identification method for a very long time, however, now people do not hesitate to present their fingerprints for unlocking their phones. The use of biometrics has been normalized as they have become part of the day-to-day life of the people. With the outbreak of coronavirus the use of biometrics has intensified. Just before the COVID-19 pandemic broke out, several groundbreaking improvements in biometric systems were announced and now there is a push to use the latest in biometrics to track people in the name of public health.

A company called WHOOP, in collaboration with Abu Dhabi-based G42 Healthcare, has launched wearable biometrics for volunteers in phase 3 trials of the coronavirus vaccine.[46] This is the first trial of its kind to feature wearable technology and will cover thousands of volunteers. It will help them self-monitor daily heart and respiratory rate, sleep performance, recovery levels and measure other key biometrics during the trials. The trials began on July 16, 2020 and are expected to last between six and twelve months.[47] Biometric body temperature scanning devices have been launched by many companies like NEC XON, Uniview and TempuCheck. NEC XON has implemented the NEC NeoFace Watch biometric facial recognition platform with its workplace monitoring solutions, along with thermal cameras for body temperature scanning.[46]

Wearable tech for recording medical data is being used in the world right now. One example of this can be found in the northern Indian state of Rajasthan, where Ruchit Nagar, a fourth-year student at Harvard Medical School and his team have devised a necklace, resembling one worn locally, which compresses, encrypts and password protects medical information.[47] The necklace uses the same technology as radio-frequency identification (RFID) chips, such as those employed in retail clothing, and provides health care workers access to a mother's pregnancy history, her child's growth chart and vaccination history, and suggestions on what vaccinations and other treatments may be needed. Such devices have reduced humans to goods. All these measures have been imposed in the name of safety of the people, workers and staff. But ultimately these devices are a new means of control and surveillance. With the development of the COVID-19 vaccine, the aim is to move towards contactless biometrics which will not require wearable tech for gathering data.

The installation of 5G technology equipment is also part of the grand biometrics scheme. On March 16th, 2020 a video surfaced on *LogicBeforeAuthority* where a whistleblower, who was a member of a local school board, gave information regarding installation of 5G equipment. [48] The school districts were intending to covertly install 5G equipment in schools during the lockdown, under the direction of the U.S. Department of Education. The companies sent in to install the 5G equipment were told to act as if they were there to disinfect the schools to stop the spread of the virus. While American Mechanical, Inc. focuses on plumbing and mechanical services, Systems Plus Wisconsin clearly states they install biometric systems and these companies were charged with the setting up of the 5G infrastructure. [49]

The COVID-19 pandemic, and the installation of biometric systems could be a part of a more sinister agenda. There are growing concerns that after the COVID-19 pandemic passes we will still be dealing with the repercussions of newly installed 5G, biometric systems, thermal imaging cameras or even temperature guns to detect who may have COVID-19. All these steps are taking us closer to a society of total surveillance where AI is constantly watching over you. The starting point of this biometric society would be the COVID-19 vaccine.

In December 2019 the researchers from MIT created an ink that can be safely embedded into the skin alongside the vaccine itself. [50] This research by MIT was funded by the Bill and Melinda Gates Foundation. It is being claimed that this 'quantum dot' can be used to track and keep records of the people who had been vaccinated and when. The COVID-19 vaccine would just be the start and the plan is to use this biometric tattoo for every vaccine so that it can cover the entire population on the planet. Along with the vaccine, a child would be injected with a bit of dye that is invisible to the naked eye but easily seen with a special cell-phone filter, combined with an app that shines near-infrared light onto the skin.[47]

The invisible "tattoo" accompanying the vaccine is a pattern made up of minuscule quantum dots–tiny semiconducting crystals that reflect light–that glows under infrared light. The dye would be expected to last up to five years, according to tests on pig and rat skin and human skin in a dish.[50] Soon enough these quantum dots will record all kinds of information and your whole life history could be revealed by a simple scan of your arm. Combining such biometrics embedded in humans with other forms of contactless biometrics, like the 5G powered facial recognition, will create a world without privacy. Mandatory vaccination will cover every person and usher us into an era of authoritarianism.

EVIDENCE PART 1: THIRD WORLD GUINEA PIGS

C LINICAL TRIALS OF THE COVID-19 vaccines are planned to be held in third-world countries. Developing countries with large populations of poor people, like India, are a perfect place to test an experimental vaccine. Apart from that, the testing of biometrics for tracking people in the name of maintaining medical records has already begun in Western Africa. The clinical trials business has gone global as drug makers seek cheaper venues for studies.[51] Big pharmaceutical companies often use people from poor and underdeveloped countries as guinea pigs for testing new medications and vaccines.

Underdeveloped countries don't have a strong legal framework to protect their people against exploitation at the hand of big corporations. These countries provide pharmaceutical companies an opportunity to test experimental drugs without the fear of serious repercussions. That is why these clinical trials lack much needed oversight and sometimes produce horrific results. In 1997, Public Citizen's Health Research Group brought widespread international attention to unethical clinical trials. The trials were testing new methods for preventing the spread of HIV infection from pregnant women to their babies before or after giving birth in developing countries in Africa, Asia and the Caribbean.[52] Most of these unethical trials were funded by the U.S. government.

There is a long history of exploitation through unethical trials as a shocking U.S. study revealed in the 1940s that several prisoners and the mentally ill were deliberately infected with syphilis in Guatemala for the conducting of vaccine trials.[51] Similarly unethical trials continue to be conducted. One recent such trial in India, reported in *The Lancet* in June, evaluated an experimental vaccine for preventing a very common, potentially life-threatening viral infection called rotavirus. The clinical trials in India were funded by multiple private and government sources, including the Bill & Melinda Gates Foundation and the National Institutes of Health.[52] These trials violated international ethical standards for conducting human research.

The Bill and Melinda Gates Foundation also funded HPV vaccine trials in India during which thousands of tribal girls were given the experimental vaccine without the informed consent of their parents or guardian. Several tribal girls suffered from seizures and died.[27] The Bill and Melinda Gates Foundation denied any such testing and the western media never reported on this story in detail. But the Indian Parliament formed a task force to investigate the unethical testing and following the inquiry the Bill and Melinda Gates Foundation was expelled from India. Annelies den Boer of the Dutch non-profit Wemos Foundation, which has been following the globalization of clinical trials since 2006, explains "People in many developing countries are often poor or illiterate, which makes them vulnerable." [51]

The Bill and Melinda Gates Foundation was at centre of another scandal in India when an oral polio vaccine backed by the Foundation caused paralysis among 496,000 children.[27]

Now the human COVID-19 vaccine trials are also proposed to be held in India. The trials were planned to start as early as July 2020. The chief of the Russian Direct Investment Fund (RDIF), Kirill Dmitriev, informed that the clinical trials of the Russian Sputnik V vaccine will be held in India.[53] The phase 3 trials of the Oxford COVID-19 vaccine are also scheduled to be held at multiple centres in India. [54]

But now this deadly game has gone much beyond vaccines. With the advent of this pandemic, the third-world countries have become testing grounds for COVID-19 vaccines coupled with biometrics for tracking and recording the public data. The blueprint for creating a world dominated by biometric surveillance with one world cashless currency and a single point of control is being tested in the underdeveloped countries. In July 2020 a public-private partnership program, backed by the Bill and Melinda Gates Foundation, between GAVI, Mastercard, and the AI identity authentication company called Trust Stamp, was ready to introduce a biometric identity platform to low-income remote communities in West Africa.[23]

It will link biometric digital identity of people to their vaccination records. The program said to "evolve as you evolve" is part of the Global War on Cash and has the potential dual use for the purposes of surveillance and "predictive policing" based on your vaccination history.[55] The program will integrate Trust Stamp's digital identity platform into the GAVI-Mastercard's "Wellness Pass", a digital vaccination record and identity system powered by Mastercard's AI and machine learning technology, NuData.[23] Those who do not wish to be vaccinated may be locked out of the system based on their trust score.

In the initial stages the plan is to deploy a new form of biometric fingerprint technology to give children, who may not even have a birth certificate, a complete medical record in order to track critical childhood vaccines. This program was actually started two years ago.[55][56] GAVI announced in June 2020 that Mastercard's Wellness Pass program has the potential to be adapted in response to the COVID-19 pandemic. Mastercard announced a month later that Trust Stamp's advanced biometric identity platform will also be integrated into the Wellness Pass. This decision was taken in the light of the Trust Stamp's capability of providing biometric identity globally, even in places lacking internet access or cellular connectivity. Trust Stamp's biometric identity program does not even require knowledge of an individual's legal name or identity to function.[55]

Evidence Part 2: The Western World's Expedited Vaccines

IN RECENT YEARS, BIG PHARMA has consistently tried to push the agenda that vaccines cannot be administered effectively unless backed up by biometrics. In 2017, Seth Berkley, GAVI chief executive officer, wrote that immunization programs are still unable to cover millions of children in developing countries, and that such efforts need "affordable, secure digital identification systems that can store a child's medical history." As technology becomes less expensive and more sophisticated, "digital" has begun to mean nothing else but "biometric".[57]

The mission to give everyone in the world some form of identification–a digital form, inevitably–has really taken off over the past decade. In 2014 the World Bank launched Identification for Development, or ID4D, a program that aims to improve access to the bank's resources in areas such as health, financial inclusion, and social welfare. In recent years, massive digital ID projects have been planned or rolled out by governments in Brazil, India, Kenya, and Nigeria.[57]

Tens of millions of Kenyans have had their faces and fingerprints digitized. India's ID authority, known as Aadhaar, reads fingerprints and irises. Most of the time, a smartphone and a small scanner are all that are needed to enroll people. These programs promise that becoming visible to the State can provide some sort of protection to individuals.

As mentioned earlier, researchers from MIT, backed by the Bill and Melinda Gates Foundation have created an ink that can be safely embedded in the skin next to the vaccine itself, that's only visible using a special smartphone camera app and filter.

This invisible "tattoo" which comes as an add-on to the vaccine is a pattern made up of minuscule quantum dots (tiny semiconducting crystals that reflect light) that glows under infrared light. The pattern and the vaccine get delivered into the skin using hi-tech dissolvable microneedles made of a mixture of polymers and sugar. When tested in human cadavers, the tattoo lasted over five years of simulated sun exposure.[50]

In other words, they've found a hidden way to insert the record of a vaccination directly into a patient's skin instead of recording it electronically or on paper–and their low-risk tracking system could significantly abridge the process of keeping accurate vaccine records, particularly on a bigger scale.

"In areas where paper vaccination cards are often lost or do not exist at all, and electronic databases are unheard of, this technology could enable the rapid and anonymous detection of patient vaccination history to ensure that every child is vaccinated," researcher Kevin McHugh said in a statement.

Since the outbreak of the latest pandemic, companies and governments have started to consider more seriously, the idea of "immunity passports," or digital IDs vouching that a person has been tested and found free of the coronavirus. In the United Kingdom a startup named Onfido that's trying to repurpose its anti-fraud technology into such passports, raised $100 million in equity financing in April.

Scott Reid, the outgoing CEO of IRespond, a Seattle-based biometric identity nonprofit, calls immunity passports "a rabbit hole that we don't want to go into. Right now, there's no consensus that having COVID-19 once gives you immunity, or for how long it gives you immunity. There are new strains that may emerge." [57]

IRespond's iris-scanning innovation has been used in medical and humanitarian settings, and Reid says it's trying to find ways to accumulate the least possible biometric data that could be linked to a vaccination record.

There have been too many recent cases of companies and governments attempting to use our personal information to monitor us and make a profit. Not surprisingly, biometrics programs have met with severe resistance in several countries. In January a court suspended Kenya's ID system because it lacked adequate data safeguards. India's Supreme Court ruled two years ago that the government couldn't force people to sign up for Aadhaar and that simple services such as opening a bank account or enrolling in a school shouldn't necessitate this biometric ID. And privacy campaigners from Hong Kong to the U.K. have protested the adoption of facial recognition technologies.

As talks about immunity passports and ID systems for vaccine tracking increased, many experts have spoken up on being extremely skeptical about this idea. In March 2020, Bill Gates held an "Ask Me Anything" session on *Reddit*, where he predicted that "eventually we will have some digital certificates to show who has recovered or been tested recently or when we have a vaccine who has received it." [58]

As we have seen, Bill Gates is already funding a program that will create everyone's digital identity based on their vaccination history. Trust Stamp is a vaccination-based digital identity program funded by Bill Gates and implemented by Mastercard and GAVI that will soon link your biometric digital identity to your vaccination records. Wellness Pass is a digital vaccination record and identity system which is to be also linked to Mastercard's click-to-play system powered by Mastercard's AI and Machine Learning technology. MasterCard made a commitment that it will create a "centralized record keeping of childhood immunization". It also describes itself as a leader towards a "World Beyond Cash".[55]

The Bill Gates digital identification program (ID 2020) presently being deployed in third-world countries have been many times likened by Christians to the Mark of the Beast. [59] [60]

There have been two realistic hypotheses since the outbreak of the novel coronavirus about the likely reasons why the government manufactured this deadly virus. Some schools of thought believe that after the pandemic has been officially declared, the next step may be – also at the recommendation of either the WHO, or individual countries – "forced vaccination" under police and/or military surveillance. Those who refuse may be penalized (fines and/or jail – and force-vaccinated all the same).[14] This is already happening.

Another hypothesis is that along with the vaccination – if not with this one, then possibly with a later one – a nanochip may be injected, unknown to the person being vaccinated. The chip may be remotely charged with all your personal data, including bank accounts and digital money. With digital money, the "one percent" could really control everything, including everyone's earnings and spending. The government would always have access to your money alongside the ability to block your access to your money, maybe as a sanction for indulging in any behavior not approved by them. Signing over the control of your money to the government is the easiest way to become a mere slave of the masters. Compared to the system of digital money, feudalism may appear like a walk in the park. Already, there are reports of new coronavirus vaccines that come in containers lined with radio-frequency identification (RFID) chips.[61]

Dr. Tedros, WHO Director-General, is already strongly advocating for the system of digital money, stating that we must move towards digital money, because physical paper and coin money can spread diseases, especially endemic diseases, like the coronavirus.

The coronavirus pandemic is apparently being used to accelerate the push for Big Brother, and tech companies are eager for an opportunity to help enforce social distancing edicts with frightening innovations. Vaccines aside, other disturbing, invasive devices are invented daily under the guise of helping save the world from the novel coronavirus.

There have been reports of FitBit-style bracelets on people in order to track them and compel certain behavior. AiRISTA Flow, a tech firm based out of Maryland, is marketing bracelets that would beep whenever a person comes within six feet of another individual in the workplace.

The Redpoint Positioning Corporation is developing similar technology to turn employers into quarantine enforcement brigades. They have announced that they are working on modifying "cutting-edge technology ... already used by leading companies worldwide in third-party logistics, auto manufacturing, and mine operation" to be used in the enforcement of social distancing edicts. They plan on tagging people and products in the workplace to allow employers to institute Draconian restrictions on the freedom of movement.[16]

Israeli surveillance firm SuperCom is repackaging services that are used on criminals to enforce home confinement on ordinary people in the workplace. They are calling their service "PureCare," and it is described as a "state-of-the-art solution for quarantine and isolation monitoring to aid government efforts in containing and limiting the reach of infectious diseases." They claim it is "a non-intrusive patient friendly system that constantly tracks patient location within buildings, vehicles and outside." [16]

Fascist Eugenics: Sterility and Depopulation?

Eugenics is an age-long practice that might not necessarily have been abandoned by many in today's society. There would always be those who advocate "improving" the human species by wanting to select those who they deem worthy to reproduce. The basis for this selection could be anything at all. Early eugenics sought to reduce human suffering by "breeding out" illness, disabilities and any other traits deemed unfavorable from the human population. People who supported the practice of eugenics in the past, mostly believed that people inherited mental health challenges, criminal inclinations and even poverty, and that these "disorders" could be bred out of the gene pool. Therefore early advocates of eugenics discouraged the people whom they deemed to be "inferior stock" from reproducing; rather they encouraged the "superior stock" to populate society.

Many countries in the world encouraged eugenics, most especially America in the first half of the 20ᵗʰ century; however Germany's Adolf Hitler came along and took the evil practice to a whole new extreme with his attempts to create a superior Aryan race. Thanks to the horrifying atrocities of Hitler and the Nazis, eugenics lost a lot of its popularity after the Second World War. Hitler is said to have given eugenics a bad name. This doesn't mean that all proponents of eugenics magically disappeared from the scene. The Rockefeller family for instance, has always been a huge proponent of eugenics. As medical technology advanced, a new form of eugenics came on the scene.

Over the years, we have witnessed the birth of modern eugenics, more popularly referred to as human genetic engineering. This concept has come a long way scientifically. Scientists promise that modern eugenics would prevent disease, cure disease or improve our bodies in some momentous way. The prospective health benefits of human gene therapy are incredible on the surface, since it promises to cure many devastating or life-threatening illnesses.

But everyone ignores the potential costs of modern eugenics and its ethics. Technology now allows people to weed out what they consider unwanted traits in their unborn children. This is done in the form of genetic testing which allows parents to recognize some diseases in their child in utero which may cause them to terminate the pregnancy.

This process is highly debated since the exact meaning of "negative traits" is open to interpretation, and a lot of people feel that everyone has the right to be born irrespective of disease, or that the laws of nature shouldn't be meddled with. This goes a long way to show that there are still individuals who want to control the size and makeup of our population, either based on physical attributes or based on their poverty level.

Capitalist elites for instance, have always sought to leverage birth control in order to manage population trends. Population control is a modern branch of eugenics for which Bill and

Melinda Gates are well known. Under the guise of charity and caring for female reproductive health, Bill and Melinda Gates have targeted the African female population for years in their bid to control the world's population.

In 2018, when a report from one of Gates' philanthropic foundations found that rapid population growth in some of Africa's poorest countries could put at risk future progress towards reducing global poverty and improving health, Gates admitted to reporters, quoted on Reuters, that the population growth in Africa is a huge challenge. Therefore it is little wonder that many do not trust that his interests lie in keeping people alive.[62]

About 1,200 girls suffered fertility disorders and autoimmune sicknesses alongside other severe side effects including death in 2014, after the Gates Foundation-funded tests of experimental HPV vaccines developed by GlaxoSmithKline (GSK) and Merck, out of 23,000 young girls in faraway Indian provinces.

After investigations by the Indian government, it was found that Gates-funded researchers responsible for the program, committed pervasive ethical violations such as compelling vulnerable village girls into the trial, pressuring parents, falsifying consent forms, and other questionable practices.[63]

According to Melinda Gates, empowerment of the female gender and its reproductive health is to be achieved via the widespread distribution of long-acting, reversible contraceptives (LARCs) — primarily injectables like the notoriously dangerous Depo-Provera (and subcutaneous implants such as Norplant). In a 2012 *Newsweek* profile, Melinda Gates described visiting remote clinics in sub-Saharan Africa where, she claims, women literally begged her for Depo-Provera injections — supposedly their only means of hiding contraceptive use from "unsupportive husbands". Injectables are ideally suited to third-world countries, she opined elsewhere, because they enable women to "receive a shot behind [their] husband's back."[64][65]

These so-called charity foundations promote LARCs over more temporary contraceptives in the name of freeing women to make responsible choices; but the real reason that people like Melinda Gates prefer these long-acting methods precisely is because they afford these poor women the least choice possible short of actual sterilization. LARCs leave a lot more control in the hands of the likes of Bill and Melinda Gates and less in the hands of women, than condoms, oral contraceptives, or traditional methods. Some of these birth control methods, such as Norplant, have been known to render women infertile for as long as five years.[64]

Until recently in India, these LARCs were being promoted as a soft form of sterilization. The country's mass sterilization programs only came to a pause after 15 women died as a result of botched tubal ligations in 2014.[66]

There is a policy of the American government, called *The Kissinger Report*. It was produced in the 1970s and discusses the implications of worldwide population growth for U.S. security and overseas interests. It explicitly states that the purpose of the foreign policy in Africa is to reduce the population and that Africa had great mineral resources. The intention is to shrink the population of Africa, so that the natives do not exhaust the natural resources, as the United States needs these resources.

As previously mentioned, in 2009 thousands of tribal girls in India were administered the HPV vaccine supposedly to prevent cervical cancer. These girls became seriously injured and there were reported deaths. The Bill and Melinda Gates Foundation, which had been responsible for these vaccines, denied that the deaths were related to the vaccines even though parents of the girls had been sure that the young girls were fine prior to taking them. Other girls reported early onset of menstrual periods, terribly painful period cramps, heavy bleeding, epileptic seizures, stomach aches and mood swings.

Many of these vaccine makers visit poorer nations in the guise of philanthropy while only just looking for humans to be used as guinea pigs for their experiments. A total of 640,000 Indian children developed Non-Polio Acute Flaccid Paralysis (NPAFP) in the years between 2000 and 2017, suggesting an additional 491,000 children above the expected number with NPAFP.

Countries like India have always been a popular testing ground for America's vaccines. The vaccine makers count it as a win-win situation if they can depopulate the world while at the same time test out their vaccines. India has already announced that COVID-19 vaccinations in the country were scheduled to commence in 2020.

The shortest time ever taken by anyone to find a vaccine for an unfamiliar disease is 7 years. The average time is 20 years. The thought of a vaccine being ready in one to one and a half years after the outbreak of a novel deadly virus is simply absurd, yet Gates claims that these vaccines are ready. Remember, there are laws that give liability protection to vaccine companies, meaning that the makers of these vaccines have absolutely nothing to lose and everything to gain if they achieve their dreams of both depopulating the world and making profit. This is a population management strategy from a few individuals who want to depopulate the world.[66]

Recently, a person in Brazil who volunteered for the medical experimentation on humans with the COVID-19 vaccine was reported to have died during clinical trials. Brazilian government officials confirmed this death to the media. The company whose vaccine is being tested in the medical experiments — AstraZ-eneca — says it will continue its experiments on the remaining human survivors which is a confirmation to the world that no deaths will stand in the way of vaccine profits, it seems.

"The volunteer died on Oct. 15," the report said. "It's not clear whether the volunteer received the placebo shot or the vaccine."[67]

If this person had died in any other context, their death would of course have been counted as a "COVID-19 death", but since they were killed by the COVID-19 vaccine, the mainstream media will claim the person received a placebo, not a live vaccine. How would the media know this, seeing as no such patient data are allowed to be released on individual patients?

Basic research ethics entail that "data on clinical research volunteers must be kept confidential, in accordance with the principles of confidentiality, human dignity, and protection of participants." This means that the media must have been lying when they reported that the vaccine trial participant was part of the placebo group.

These greedy scientists would continue the experiments not-withstanding how many people die in the process.

"We cannot comment on individual cases in an ongoing trial of the Oxford vaccine as we adhere strictly to medical confiden-tiality and clinical trial regulations, but we can confirm that all required review processes have been followed," said AstraZeneca in a public statement.

All this goes a long way to show the dangerous side effects linked to coronavirus vaccines. On Sept. 8, 2020 the company had announced that its vaccine trial was placed on hold due to an illness in a patient in the United Kingdom. The Food and Drug Administration also once placed a late-stage clinical trial from AstraZeneca on hold in the United States.

Natural News recently reported how Johnson & Johnson was forced to halt another coronavirus vaccine trial after a trial participant experienced an "unexplained illness." As that story explained:

"Johnson & Johnson is pausing its Wuhan coronavirus (COVID-19) vaccine trial after a study participant fell ill. The halt comes just weeks after the company announced that they were in the final stage of the trials."

In its news release, Johnson & Johnson said that the trial was paused in compliance with regulatory standards after the unnamed participant developed an "unexplained illness".

Similarly, nine people have died in South Korea after receiving flu shots there, causing a nationwide panic over the "death vaccines" that are killing so many people so quickly. This has of course raised concerns over the vaccine's safety just as the seasonal inoculation program is expanded to head off potential COVID-19 complications.

As expected, health authorities denied these occurrences, insisting that the vaccines didn't kill anyone, since the dead people had "underlying health conditions", which is exactly what critics had warned would be said about vaccine deaths as the body count started to accelerate. It is worth noting that, when people with underlying health conditions die with a coronavirus infection, they are said to have died from COVID-19. But when they have underlying health conditions and are found dead after receiving a vaccine injection, health authorities claim the vaccine isn't related to their death.[68]

The foul play is becoming apparent. If humans are dying in a carefully controlled vaccine trial only administered to healthy individuals, how much worse would the death toll get when these hastily made vaccines are unleashed on the entire world population, a large part of which is unhealthy thanks to genetically modified foods and an environment tainted by 5G radiation?

This is clearly the quickest way for globalists to exterminate people who fail to realize the COVID-19 agenda is actually an extermination agenda targeting the human race. Fortunately, those who are intelligent enough to want to survive should be steering clear of all vaccines and vaccine industry medical experiments carried out on humans.[68]

DNA: Re-engineering Humanity in the Image of Artificial Intelligence

To be sure, tension between privacy and biometric technologies began long before the COVID-19 pandemic. Concerns over government usage of forms of biometric surveillance, including facial recognition, surfaced as technology proliferated at airports, border checkpoints, and with police body cameras. The same technology is now causing similar concerns as other countries – China, for example – are using facial recognition to enforce compliance with quarantine orders and to detect pedestrians' body temperatures in crowds. Indeed, advances in biometric technologies now allow the ability to recognize individuals even if they are wearing masks, and biometric identification systems can offer "non-refutable" proof of antibodies by linking test subjects to results, which could enable a more targeted approach to vaccines, once available. This could prove to be of tremendous value to U.S. companies.

While they had everyone locked up indoors afraid of the pandemic, there were reports of ongoing installation of 5G towers.[69]

There's a major concern that 5G could be installed without our knowledge while we are grappling with the fallout of the COVID-19 pandemic, and that the installation of biometric systems could be a part of a more sinister agenda.

Namely, we are concerned that after the COVID-19 pandemic passes we will still be dealing with the repercussions of newly installed 5G, biometric systems, thermal imaging cameras or even temperature guns to detect who MAY have COVID-19.

Even more worrisome is the idea of government-mandated vaccinations; and, for example, that only those who can prove they have received the COVID-19 vaccine (once it's developed) will be allowed back to work, school, public parks, public transportation, etc.

This is even more worrisome when you consider that Bill Gates – a longtime proponent of vaccinations and population control – recently stated:

"Eventually we will have some digital certificates to show who has recovered or been tested recently or when we have a vaccine who has received it."

What does Gates mean by a "digital certificate"? Could it be tied in to the Global ID2020 or the discussion of a "tattoo" that tells the medical authorities whether you have been vaccinated, for example?

Totalitarianism through Technology

D AVID ICKE, SPEAKING FURTHER ON the truth behind the
COVID-19 pandemic and the resulting economic crash
explains that there is a cult at the core of the government
in many countries. The cult is trying to create a beyond Orwellian
world system in which a very few extremely rich people dictate
to everyone else. He calls this a "Hunger Games Society". Picture
this Society as a pyramid, where the controlling party is at the
top of the pyramid. This controlling party is also known as "the
one percent".[35]

The rest of the world is at the bottom of this pyramid all
answering to the one percent. In between both parties is a vicious,
merciless, police military state, to enforce the will of "the one
percent" on the people and prevent them from revolting. This
Hunger Games Society is not classic fascism or communism, it
is a technocracy.

A technocracy is a society controlled by bureaucrats, scientists,
engineers, and experts. This kind of society can only happen
through smart technology and AI. The idea is that everything,
even the human brain, would be connected through AI. This

means that whoever controls AI, would be able to control everyone's perception of reality. This controlling would be done from a central point – a global point grid.

At the moment, the cult is working hard to ensure the creation of this society using two major techniques. The first technique is the Problem-Reaction-Solution technique discussed earlier. The second technique is what Icke calls the "totalitarian tiptoe". The totalitarian tiptoe can best described as a situation where the government starts off at point A and knows right away that they're headed to point Z. They also know that if they take too big a leap to point Z, the public is going to start asking questions. So they take the biggest steps possible towards their goal, but never take so big a step that the public becomes worried, making everyone believe that all strange occurrences are completely random and not calculated steps towards the big goal.

However, as the phrase goes, "know the outcome and you'll see the journey", and the same applies to this scenario. If you don't know the intended outcome of the government, all of the recent events would appear completely random, i.e., the pandemic and the resultant economic crises. For years, unhealthy genetically modified foods have been pumped into the system, people have breathed in extremely polluted air, and dangerous electromagnetic waves installed by unchecked tech companies have surrounded us. All of these factors have worn down the immune systems of members of the public, especially the elderly. Since the outbreak of the pandemic, we've been asked to wear masks and stay indoors, but nothing has been done to boost the immune systems of the elderly and inform, engage in focused protection, or clean up the environment.

This shows that the aim of the people in power is not to keep the world safe from the virus but to dismantle the world's economic system. There's been indisputable evidence that the risk of dying from the COVID-19 virus is exceedingly low for young people with no underlying health conditions, so why are young healthy business owners still asked to lock up their businesses and remain indoors? The Hunger Games Society is designed to have no small or medium scale businesses; these are the businesses that have been targeted in the fake pandemic. As the businesses fold up, the business owners join the poor at the bottom of the pyramid.

The cult could not have achieved this with physical force, so they seek to control the rest of the population through controlling the information. They continually disseminate information that threatens their jobs, survival, loved ones etc. This way, survival mechanisms–where people engage in absurd behaviors to survive – kick in. An example is fighting over toilet paper at the grocery store, even though it made little to no sense to be that concerned over toilet paper at the beginning of a pandemic. Icke insists that a brain in survival mode would agree to anything, no matter how Draconian, as long as it perceives that "anything" as an aid to its survival.

The pandemic kicking in your survival mechanism means that not only will you accept the authorities imposing tyranny to keep you safe; it means that you'll also demand that the authorities enforce tyranny on others who refuse to co-operate. This way, governments have managed to make COVID-19 vaccines compulsory even though these vaccines have not been fully tested and their effects are not fully known. Worse still, because of the Vaccine Act, vaccine makers are protected by the government against liability from vaccine damage or death. This means that humans are basically being used as lab rats for profit. You may think that the government is doing this for the greater good, but if this were the case, there would be measures to keep the elderly safe and build up their immunity while the young and strong go back to normal life. But all the policies currently in existence only aim to further the government's agenda of creating a totalitarian world.

COVID-19 is the perfect Trojan horse for a control freak State itching to not only micromanage the lives of ordinary citizens but also ferret out critics and potential adversaries and punish them as enemies of the State. The latter is the primary objective. History is replete with examples—from Stalin and Mao to Hitler and Mussolini, with lesser autocrats and dictators along the way. [11]

"What they really want is a fully standardized data collection and retrieval format, and cross-border sharing of identities of the entire population of the planet, in order for the stand-alone AI-powered command center to work without a hitch, and for purposes of calculating everyone's potential contribution, and threat to the system." [70]

If you believe this is dangerously close to China's "social credit" system, you're not far off the mark.

Introducing this totalitarian technology under the cover of a supposed pandemic rife with speculation and a dearth of hard numbers is a near-perfect cover for "patient ID technology" producing data on individuals shared with the State and its corporate partners.

A vaccine ostensibly designed to combat COVID-19 will become mandatory and those who resist will be blacklisted as public health criminals. They will be locked out of society, similar to Chinese citizens suffering under China's totalitarian social credit system.

Presently, China uses a system of AI to track all its citizens and their everyday behaviors. Then they use a social credit system to reward good behavior and punish bad behavior. Needless to say that good and bad behavior is dictated by the State. Many citizens who behaved in ways found unacceptable by the State have been banned from flying or attending trainings, etc. China is currently practicing a technocracy, and like everything it's done since the pandemic, the rest of the world will follow suit.

Presently, LifeQ, a manufacturer of wearable devices containing health information and biometrics, is to supply its COVID-19 early warning and disease tracking device to Southern Africa. The company claims they designed the device "to help companies get back to business safely in the midst of the global pandemic, allowing businesses to predict outbreaks and assist employees towards recovery."

LifeQ's so-called personalized anomaly detector, works by analyzing a range of continuous physiological streams to spot the onset of illnesses like COVID-19 even before symptoms are displayed. It also monitors progression of the illness to help triage for medical intervention.[71]

Transhumanism: The Ultimate Evil

Looking at the world's governance for years, one will notice that there is a permanent government (the cult) and a temporal government which is the present leader you see in every country, here today, gone tomorrow (Donald Trump, Barack Obama, Boris Johnson, Jinping Xi). The temporary governments are usually just tools used to push the agenda of the cult. Even times when the temporary figureheads have a different viewpoint from the cult, they are manipulated into doing the bidding of the cult by constantly being asked how they want to be remembered in the future. This is the scenario that has played out with the entire handling of the pandemic and now with the rushed vaccines.[35]

Carrie Madej, an osteopathic internal medicine physician in Georgia discusses the implications of rushed vaccines in an alarming video that considers recent scientists' attempts to explore transhumanism. The transhumanist movement seeks to liberate the human race from its biological constraints; melding human intelligence with AI and bestowing humanity with superpowers.[72]

Anyone who's ever seen a sci-fi movie must have imagined what it would be like if technology ever came to this in the real world. Well, technology has indeed come to this. The proposed COVID-19 vaccine is nothing like the world has ever experienced and contains features that can change who we are very quickly, says Dr. Madej.

Famous scientists Elon Musk and Ray Kurzweil are self-proclaimed transhumanists who believe that humans should be improved from Human 1.0 to Human 2.0. There are huge proponents of this belief among other scientists.[73]

One of the front runners for the COVID-19 vaccine is Moderna, founded by Harvard scientist Derek Rossi. Rossi took RNA from the body, modified it, and using it was able to reprogram a stem cell in the body, changing its function so that it became genetically improved. He proved that you can genetically modify anyone by using modified RNA.[72]

Moderna was founded based on this new technology, which had never been used in any previous medicines or vaccines for humans. The company itself had no previous experience with finding and manufacturing vaccines. The COVID-19 virus was the perfect excuse for Moderna to try it for the first time. The experimental vaccine has gone from phases 1 to 3 during the period from March 2020 to the present day. This pace is awfully fast as normal vaccine development takes about five years to get to this stage.

Moderna, like other vaccine companies, is fast-tracking its research. How are they able to work this fast and still take responsibility for all the safety precautions required? In the Moderna COVID-19 test study, only 45 humans were tested. With the high dose vaccine test group, 100% of the participants experienced systematic side effects. With the low dose group, 80% had systematic side effects. Needless to say, these figures are terrible and spell disaster for the human race.

More still, the long-term side effects of the vaccine are still unknown and won't be known for years, but from previous similar studies, one can expect increased cancer rates, increased autoimmune reactions and other similar reactions. In ferret studies, it was noticed that when the virus was introduced to the ferrets after the vaccine, they had an exaggerated immune response, lung inflammation, lung fluid and liver problems.

With these vaccines, there is an idea called a microneedle platform developed by MIT scientists. This idea makes it easy to mass-produce vaccines which could be self-administered. The vaccines look like a band-aid which could be bought at any drugstore, online or offline. One can stick this on their arm then take it off just like a band-aid and they would be vaccinated.

How is this possible? The band-aid has little tiny needles (the "microneedles") designed like snake viper fangs, therefore it's like little snake bites. Inside these needles, you'll find some hydrogel; this hydrogel will contain luciferase enzymes as well as the vaccine itself.

So when you inject yourself with this vaccine, you will also be getting modified RNA. The idea behind this modified RNA is that the microneedles would puncture your cell membrane and stimulate your body to make more of the virus. The idea is for your body to get accustomed to the virus so that in the future, the body would know how to make antibodies that have a better response to the virus.

The problem with this idea is that it's based on a process called transfection. Transfection is the same process used in making genetically modified organisms, and can result in unexpected morphologies and abnormalities in target cells. For instance, the genetically modified fruits and vegetables you get at the mall were created using transfection and are usually not as healthy as the normal fruits and vegetables. If humans become genetically modified, who is to say that the same wouldn't apply?

Vaccine manufacturers constantly assure the public that genetically modified humans would not be weaker than normal humans; however what is the proof that this is true? By definition, transfection could be permanent or temporary. Vaccine manufacturers are hoping that the vaccine only causes a temporary change but what happens when it causes a permanent change?

Whether the change is permanent or temporary, we may never be completely sure until several years down the road. There's a possibility that this vaccine could alter the human genome. If these synthetic patented vaccines alter our genome, do we somehow become the property of the people whose patents live inside us and control our behavior? These are questions to ask before taking such vaccines, says Dr. Madej.

The luciferase enzyme found inside the vaccine has the job of keeping track of the vaccinated and their vaccination records. An app on your phone used to scan the area where you were vaccinated would show your vaccination records and an ID number. You will be no different from any other product.

The hydrogel contained in the vaccine is an invention of the Defense Advanced Research Projects Agency (*DARPA*). It is a nanotechnology made up of microscopic little robots. It is AI and has the ability to connect with other AI. This would take away one's freedom and autonomy because anyone would be able to gather data on you at any time including such information as your rate of motion, menstrual cycle and medicine intake. Humans can send and receive information with their bodies if this technology is inside them. How are we protected from the future misuse of this information? More importantly, at what point do we go from being human to superhuman?

It's important to know that over a hundred COVID-19 vaccines are still in development and would take years to complete, so we must beware of these vaccines that have magically become ready in a jiffy. These ones that come with a biometric tattoo are here to accomplish the plan of forcing things into your body that then slowly debilitate you with binary weapon systems and kill you.[9] If you carefully observe every development that's been reported in the mainstream media since the onset of this pandemic, it would be quite apparent that the COVID-19 virus was created to usher in a world of new tech, including robots, biometrics and AI to the detriment of the human race.[74]

In 1986, President Ronald Reagan signed the National Childhood Vaccine Injury Act granting total immunity to vaccine companies. It all started after a decade of lawsuits related to vaccine injuries and deaths, and vaccine makers were going bankrupt. In a bid to coax lawmakers, vaccine makers threatened to stop making vaccines until they could be legally shielded from liability. So to this day, if someone is injured or dies from a vaccine, the U.S. taxpayers pay the compensation.

CONCLUSION

A N APRIL 2020 SURVEY DONE in the USA found that nearly a third of Americans say they'll refuse a COVID-19 vaccine if it becomes available.[5] These people have understood that in today's tech-led world, a biometric vaccine would mean giving up your basic human rights to freedom of movement, the right to privacy, and emerging data rights as these vaccines are made to be highly invasive, so that they would achieve their only objective–establishing the New World Order.

Such invasive methods include tracking apps, facial recognition technology, tracing credit card transactions, using cell phone information, video footage and public posting of detailed information of the sick. Needless to say, this would create a dreadful world to live in. For one, we live in an age of data insecurity when companies and even governments are constantly looking to use every bit of our personal information they can access to monetize and monitor us. The world government desperately needs this data for the sinister agenda that has been discussed in this book.

For this reason, more people must be prepared to say no to the COVID-19 biometric vaccine. Before you give away your basic human rights in exchange for a COVID-19 vaccine, you must remember the following. Firstly, the WHO has said that about 80% of people with COVID-19 have few to no symptoms. This means you could have the virus in your body and not even be aware of it, especially if you are young and have no underlying health conditions. Secondly, the mortality rate from the virus is highly exaggerated. The CDC has instructed health workers to list COVID-19 as the cause of death, even if it isn't a person's main or only cause of death. The numbers of positives are also greatly exaggerated, due to unreliable and hastily manufactured test kits. Remember that in Tanzania a goat, vehicle oil, and fruit tested positive for COVID-19 in the thick of the pandemic.[75]

The COVID-19 virus has proved to be the perfect crisis to justify and enforce any kind of agenda. The world governments have cashed in on this situation to push plans including but not limited to totalitarianism through technology, transhumanism and even eugenics. This evil agenda will only be thwarted if more people say "no" to the COVID-19 biometric vaccine.

References

1. Sørensen, B., Susrud, A., & Dalgleish, A. (2020). Biovacc-19: A Candidate Vaccine for COVID-19 (SARS-CoV-2) Developed from Analysis of its General Method of Action for Infectivity. *QRB Discovery*, 1, E6. doi:10.1017/qrd.2020.8

2. Coutard, B., Valle, C., de Lamballerie, X., Canard, B., Seidah, N.G., Decroly, E. (2020) The spike glycoprotein of the new coronavirus 2019-nCoV contains a furin-like cleavage site absent in CoV of the same clade. *Antiviral Research*, 176 (104742), ISSN 0166-3542. *https://doi.org/10.1016/j.antiviral.2020.104742*

3. Zhan, S.H., Deverman, B.E., Chan, Y.A., (2020) SARS-CoV-2 is well adapted for humans. What does this mean

for re-emergence? *bioRxiv*, 2020.05.01.073262. *https://doi.org/10.1101/2020.05.01.073262*

4. Technology threatens human rights in the coronavirus fight. (May 7, 2020). Retrieved from *https://theconversation.com/technology-threatens-human-rights-in-the-coronavirus-fight-136159*

5. Biometric Tracking Can Ensure Billions Have Immunity Against COVID-19. (August 13, 2020). Retrieved from *https://www.bloomberg.com/features/2020-covid-vaccine-tracking-biometric/*

6. Breggin, P.R. & Breggin, G.R. (2020) Dr. Fauci's COVID-19 Treachery with Chilling Ties to the Chinese Military. Retrieved from *https://vaccineliberationarmy.com/wp-content/uploads/2020/10/COVID-19-the-blog-TREACHERY-WITH-ANTHONY-FAUCI.pdf*

7. Dr. Breggin's Resume and Bibliography. Retrieved from *https://breggin.com/*

8. Health Checkpoints, Biometric IDs, Vaccine Ink Injections: Media Reveals Orwellian 'New Normal' on the Horizon Due to COVID-19. (July 30, 2020). Retrieved from *https://bigleaguepolitics.com/health-checkpoints-biometric-ids-vaccine-ink-injections-media-reveals-orwellian-new-normal-on-the-horizon-due-to-covid-19/*

9. Why Americans Fear the COVID-19 Vaccine. (August 19, 2020). Retrieved from *https://healthylife-pro.blogspot.com/2020/08/why-americans-fear-covid-19-vaccine.html*

10. COVID-19 Vaccine Trial Gets Support from Biometric Wristband. (August 17, 2020). Retrieved from *https://mobileidworld.com/covid-19-vaccine-trial-support-biometric-wristband-081705/*

11. COVID-19: Perfect Cover for Mandatory Biometric ID. (April 9, 2020). Retrieved from *https://www.theburning platform.com/2020/04/09/covid-19-perfect-cover-for-mandatory-biometric-id/*

12. Micro-Chipped New World Order 4 of 4. (May 8, 2020). Retrieved from *https://pressingforadams.wordpress.com/2020/05/08/micro-chipped-new-world-order-3/*

13. Bill Gates develops 'digital certificates' for Coronavirus. (March 29, 2020). Retrieved from *https://www.parlayme.com/post/bill-gates-develops-digital-certificates-for-coronavirus*

14. The Coronavirus COVID-19 Pandemic: The Real Danger is "Agenda ID2020". (Updated November 21, 2020 from March 12, 2020 original). Retrieved from *https://www.globalresearch.ca/coronavirus-causes-effects-real-danger-agenda-id2020/5706153*

15. Biometric IDs can be 'gamechanger' in coronavirus antibody tests, vaccine. (April, 8 2020). Retrieved from *https://uk.reuters.com/article/health-coronavirus-tech/biometric-ids-can-be-gamechanger-in-coronavirus-antibody-tests-vaccine-idUKL8N-2BV0BI*

16. Health Checkpoints, Biometric IDs, Vaccine Ink Injections: Media Reveals Orwellian 'New Normal' on the Horizon Due to COVID-19. (August 1, 2020). Retrieved from *https://www.sgtreport.com/2020/08/health-checkpoints-biometric-ids-vaccine-ink-injections-media-reveals-orwellian-new-normal-on-the-horizon-due-to-covid-19/*

17. Coronavirus: Could biometric ID cards offer the UK a lockdown exit strategy? (April 10, 2020). Retrieved from *https://ca.news.yahoo.com/coronavirus-could-biometric-id-cards-offer-uk-lockdown-134000739.html?guccounter=1*

18. UK Introduces Biometric Enabled Coronavirus Digital Health Passports. (2020). Retrieved November 8, 2020 from

https://tichronicles.com/2020/05/28/covi-pass-uk-introdu-ces-biometric-rfid-enabled-coronavirus-digital-health-pass-ports/?fbclid=IwAR2Bci2SPIIB8iSXmeUrZJSot1AX281gvb-w5x99z4wUALPrnQiGXXetC1To

19. Platform for biometric ID COVID-19 immunity passport. (June 17, 2020). Electronicspecifier.com. Retrieved November 8, 2020 from *https://www.electronicspecifier.com/industries/medical/platform-for-biometric-id-covid-19-immunity-passport-1*

20. COVID-19 Spurs Facial Recognition Tracking, Privacy Fears. (March 20, 2020). Threatpost.com. Retrieved November 8, 2020 from *https://threatpost.com/covid-19-spurs-facial-recognition-tracking-privacy-fears/153953/*

21. Nunn, A. (2020). Biometrics and Coronavirus: Balancing Promise With Privacy. Autho Blog. Retrieved November 8, 2020 from *https://autho.com/blog/biometrics-and-coronavirus-balancing-promise-with-privacy/*

22. Tracking and tracing COVID: Protecting privacy and data while using apps and biometrics. (April 23, 2020). OECD. Retrieved November 8, 2020, from *http://www.oecd.org/coronavirus/policy-responses/tracking-and-tracing-covid-protecting-privacy-and-data-while-using-apps-and-biomet-rics-8f394636/*

23. Public-private partnership launches biometrics identity and vaccination record system in West Africa. (July 10, 2020). Privacy International. Retrieved November 8, 2020 from *https://privacyinternational.org/examples/4083/public-private-part-nership-launches-biometrics-identity-and-vaccination-rec-ord-system*

24. Testing Will Begin In Africa For Biometric ID, "Vaccine Records", & "Payment Systems". (July 17, 2020). Retrieved November 8, 2020 from *https://www.zerohedge.com/markets/*

testing-will-begin-africa-biometric-id-vaccine-records-pay-ment-systems

25. Trust Stamp integrating biometric hash solution with Master-card on children's vaccine record system. (July 6, 2020). Biometric Update. Retrieved November 8, 2020 from *https://www.biometricupdate.com/202007/trust-stamp-integrating-biometric-hash-solution-with-mastercard-on-childrens-vaccine-record-system*

26. Neuralink: Elon Musk unveils pig with chip in its brain. (August 29, 2020). BBC News. Retrieved November 8, 2020 from *https://www.bbc.com/news/world-us-canada-53956683*

27. Plandemic: Indoctornation World Premiere. (August 18, 2020). Digital Freedom Platform by London Real. Retrieved November 8, 2020 from *https://freedomplatform.tv/plandemic-indoctornation-world-premiere/*

28. PROBLEM-REACTION-SOLUTION. (2020) Anythingbox.wordpress.com. Retrieved November 8, 2020 from *https://anythingbox.wordpress.com/2009/03/24/problem-reaction-solution/*

29. Coronavirus: David Icke's channel deleted by *YouTube*. (May 2, 2020). BBC News. Retrieved November 8, 2020 from *https://www.bbc.com/news/technology-52517797*

30. Coronavirus: David Icke kicked off Facebook. (May 1, 2020). BBC News. Retrieved November 8, 2020 from *https://www.bbc.com/news/technology-52501453*

31. Scenarios for the Future of Technology and International Development. (May 2020). The Rockefeller Foundation and Global Business Network. Retrieved November 8, 2020 from *http://www.nommeraadio.ee/meedia/pdf/RRS/Rockefeller%20Foundation.pdf*

32. Conspiracy Theory with Jesse Ventura | Police State. (2016). Dailymotion video. Retrieved November 8, 2020 from *https://www.dailymotion.com/video/x4j66oe*

33. Dr. Li-Meng Yan: Coronavirus Whistleblower–How the Chinese Government Covered Up the Emergence of the SARS COV-2 Virus. (September 25, 2020). Digital Freedom Platform by London Real. Retrieved November 8, 2020 from *https://freedomplatform.tv/dr-li-meng-yan-coronavirus-whistleblower-how-the-chinese-government-covered-up-the-emergence-of-the-sars-cov-2-*

34. New World War: The New Enemy. (2020). Newworldwar.org. Retrieved November 8, 2020 from *http://www.newworldwar.org/newenemy.htm*

35. The Truth Behind The Coronavirus Pandemic, COVID-19 Lockdown & The Economic Crash–David Icke. (March 18, 2020). Digital Freedom Platform by London Real. Retrieved November 8, 2020 from *https://freedomplatform.tv/the-truth-behind-the-coronavirus-pandemic-covid-19-lockdown-the-economic-crash-david-icke/*

36. Coronavirus: WHO reports record daily rise in new infections. (September 14, 2020). BBC News. Retrieved November 8, 2020 from *https://www.bbc.com/news/world-54142502*

37. Denmark rushes through emergency coronavirus law. (March 13, 2020). Thelocal.dk. Retrieved November 8, 2020 from *https://www.thelocal.dk/20200313/denmark-passes-far-reaching-emergency-coronavirus-law*

38. China's social credit system bares its teeth, banning millions from taking flights, trains. (February 18, 2019). South China Morning Post. Retrieved November 8, 2020 from *https://www.scmp.com/economy/china-economy/article/2186606/chinas-social-credit-system-shows-its-teeth-banning-millions*

39. Biometric Authentication Now and Then: History and Timeline. (2020). Bayometric. Retrieved November 8, 2020 from *https://www.bayometric.com/biometric-authentication-history-timeline/*

40. History of Biometrics. (2012). Biometricupdate.com. Retrieved November 8, 2020 from *https://www.biometricupdate.com/201802/history-of-biometrics-2*

41. Pike, J. Biometrics–History. (2020). Globalsecurity.org. Retrieved November 8, 2020 from *https://www.globalsecurity.org/security/systems/biometrics-history.htm*

42. How to Use Android Phone As Biometric Device. (December 18, 2018). M2SYS Blog on Biometric Technology. Retrieved November 8, 2020 from *https://www.m2sys.com/blog/biometric-hardware/how-to-use-android-phone-as-biometric-device/*

43. Dudley, Lauren. (March 7, 2020). China's Ubiquitous Facial Recognition Tech Sparks Privacy Backlash. Thediplomat.com. Retrieved November 8, 2020 from *https://thediplomat.com/2020/03/chinas-ubiquitous-facial-recognition-tech-sparks-privacy-backlash/#:~:text=As%20the%20number%20of%20facial,the%20security%20of%20sensitive%20data*

44. 6 Ways Amazon Uses Big Data To Stalk You. (October 5, 2020). Investopedia. Retrieved November 8, 2020 from *https://www.investopedia.com/articles/insights/090716/7-ways-amazon-uses-big-data-stalk-you-amzn.asp*

45. Biometrics in 2020 (FAQs, use cases, technology). (2020). Thalesgroup.com. Retrieved November 8, 2020 from *https://www.thalesgroup.com/en/markets/digital-identity-and-security/government/inspired/biometrics*

46. Biometrics and body temperature scanning technologies support COVID-19 recovery efforts. (August 17, 2020). Biometricupdate.com. Retrieved November 8, 2020 from *https://www.biometricupdate.com/202008/biometrics-and-body-temperature-scanning-technologies-support-covid-19-recovery-efforts*

47. COVID-19: Wearable technology to help vaccine trial volunteers track fitness. (August 14, 2020). Khaleej Times. Retrieved 8 November 2020 from *https://www.khaleejtimes.com/coronavirus-pandemic/covid-19-wearable-technology-to-help-vaccine-trial-volunteers-track-fitness*

48. Weintraub, K. (December 18, 2019). Invisible Ink Could Reveal whether Kids Have Been Vaccinated. Scientific American. Retrieved November 8, 2020 from *https://www.scientificamerican.com/article/invisible-ink-could-reveal-whether-kids-have-been-vaccinated/*

49. Are 5G/Biometric Systems Being Covertly Installed During the Lockdown, Where You Live? (2020) The Deidre Imus Environmental Health Center. Imusenvironmentalhealth.org. Retrieved November 8, 2020 from *http://www.imusenvironmentalhealth.org/are-5gbiometric-systems-being-covertly-installed-during-the-lockdown-where-you-live/*

50. Tangermann, Victor. (December 21, 2019). An Invisible Quantum Dot 'Tattoo' Could Be Used to ID Vaccinated Kids. ScienceAlert. Retrieved November 8, 2020 from *https://www.sciencealert.com/an-invisible-quantum-dot-tattoo-is-being-suggested-to-id-vaccinated-kids*

51. Hirschler, Ben. (May 6, 2011). Special report: Big Pharma's global guinea pigs. London (Reuters). Retrieved November 8, 2020 from *https://in.reuters.com/article/us-pharmaceut-*

icals-trials/special-report-big-pharmas-global-guinea-pigs-idUKTRE7450SV20110506

52. Unethical Clinical Trials Still Being Conducted in Developing Countries. (October 1, 2014). Public Citizen. Retrieved November 8, 2020 from *https://www.citizen.org/news/unethical-clinical-trials-still-being-conducted-in-developing-countries/*

53. 'Russian COVID vaccine to be tested in India this month'. (September 7, 2020). The Tribune.Tribune India News Service. Retrieved November 8, 2020 from *https://www.tribuneindia.com/news/nation/russian-covid-vaccine-to-be-tested-in-india-this-month-137755*

54. Coronavirus Vaccine India: Phase III Human Trials Of Oxford COVID Vaccine To Start In Mumbai. (August 19, 2020). The Times of India. Timesofindia.com. Retrieved November 8, 2020 from *https://timesofindia.indiatimes.com/life-style/health-fitness/health-news/coronavirus-vaccine-india-phase-iii-human-trials-of-oxford-covid-vaccine-to-start-in-mumbai/photostory/77631522.cms?picid=77631538*

55. Trust Stamp–Bill Gates Funded Program That Will Create Your Digital Identity Based On Your Vaccination History. (July 19, 2020). GreatGameIndia–Journal on Geopolitics & International Relations. Retrieved November 8, 2020 from *https://greatgameindia.com/bill-gates-vaccination-based-digital-identity/*

56. Schlesinger, D. (July 6, 2019). New Gavi Partnership: Deploying Biometric Technology To Expand Child Vaccine Coverage. Health Policy Watch. Retrieved November 8, 2020 from *https://healthpolicy-watch.news/new-gavi-partnership-deploying-biometric-technology-to-expand-child-vaccine-coverage/*

57. Biometric Tracking Can Ensure Billions Have Immunity Against COVID-19 (August 13, 2020). Retrieved from *https://www.bloomberg.com/features/2020-covid-vaccine-tracking-biometric/*

58. I'm Bill Gates, co-chair of the Bill & Melinda Gates Foundation. AMA about COVID-19 (2020). Retrieved October 24, 2020 from *https://www.reddit.com/r/Coronavirus/comments/fksnbf/im_bill_gates_cochair_of_the_bill_melinda_gates/*

59. THE MARK OF THE BEAST IS AT THE DOOR – ID2020 Implants – Vaccines. (April 9, 2020). Retrieved October 2, 2020 from *https://www.eyeopeningtruth.com/the-mark-of-the-beast-is-at-the-door-id-implants-vaccines/*

60. MARK OF THE BEAST–HERE IT COMES: Bill Gates And His GAVI Vaccine Alliance Launching AI-Powered 'Trust Stamp' Combining A Vaccine And Digital Biometric ID In West Africa. (July 14, 2020). Retrieved from *https://nevrapture.blogspot.com/2020/07/mark-of-beast-here-it-comes-bill-gates.html*

61. RFID Chip May Be Tied to the New Coronavirus Vaccine (May 22, 2020). Retrieved from *https://www1.cbn.com/cbnnews/health/2020/may/rfid-chip-may-be-tied-to-the-new-coronavirus-vaccine*

62. Africa's rapid population growth puts poverty progress at risk, says Gates (September 18, 2018). Retrieved from *https://uk.reuters.com/article/uk-health-global-gates/africas-rapid-population-growth-puts-poverty-progress-at-risk-says-gates-idUKKCN1LYoGQ*

63. Bill Gates Is Not a Benign Philanthropist, Quite the Contrary. (August 22, 2018). Retrieved from *http://www.newdemocracy-world.org/culture/gates.html*

64. Bill Gates and the Myth of Overpopulation. (April 26, 2019). Retrieved from *https://medium.com/@jacob.levich/ bill-gates-and-the-myth-of-overpopulation-ca3b1d89680*

65. Melinda Gates reinvesting in Family Planning with Depo Provera. (2020) Retrieved from *https://www.occupycorporatism. com/melinda-gates-reinvesting-in-family-planning-with-depo-provera*

66. India to Change Its Decades-Old Reliance on Female Sterilization. (February 20, 2016). Retrieved from *https://www. nytimes.com/2016/02/21/world/asia/india-to-change-its-dec-ades-old-reliance-on-female-sterilization.html*

67. Volunteer in COVID-19 Vaccine Trial Dies: Health Officials. (September 3, 2020). Retrieved from *https://www.theepoch-times.com/volunteer-in-covid-19-vaccine-trial-dies-in-health-officials_3547777.html*

68. 3 CRITICAL COVID VIDEOS (2020). Retrieved from *https:// stateofthenation.co/?page_id=31131*

69. Are 5G / Biometric Systems Being Covertly Installed During the Lockdown, Where You Live? (March 22, 2020). Retrieved from *https://www.globalresearch.ca/are-5g-biometric-sys-tems-being-covertly-installed-during-lockdown-where-you-live/5707159*

70. ID2020 Alliance: Global Mandatory Vaccinations + Biometric ID Integration. (December 20, 2019). Retrieved from *https://eclinik.net/id2020-alliance-global-mandatory-vaccina-tions-biometric-id-integration/*

71. Wearable COVID-19 tracker available in Southern Africa. (September 3, 2020). Retrieved from *https:// www.healthcareglobal.com/medical-devices-and-pharma/ wearable-covid-19-tracker-available-southern-africa*

72. Dr. Carrie Mandej warns of the nanotechnology used in the rushed vaccine. (September, 1, 2020). Retrieved from *https://www.bitchute.com/video/KjFRsu61fdiX/*

73. Human 2.0 is coming faster than you think. Would you evolve with the times? (October 1, 2018). Retrieved from *https://www.forbes.com/sites/cognitiveworld/2018/10/01/human-2-0-is-coming-faster-than-you-think-will-you-evolve-with-the-times/?sh=4040e0c44284*

74. Coronavirus is the first big test for futuristic tech that can prevent pandemics. (February 27, 2020). Retrieved from *https://www.vox.com/recode/2020/2/27/21156358/surveillance-tech-coronavirus-china-facial-recognition*

75. Coronavirus COVID-19 666 Mark of the Beast Bible Prophecy, Vaccinations & Cryptocurrency. (May 4, 2020). Retrieved from *https://hackernoon.com/covid-19-and-the-bibles-666-prophecy-zb2432po*

APPENDIX A-1

The Subpoena is Technically Deficient

7. The Justice of the Peace did not have jurisdiction to issue the subpoena under s. 34(3) of the ~~Alberta Evidence Act, RSA~~ 18, and it should be quashed on this basis.

The CMOH Has No Material Evidence

8. Mr. King has no evidence showing that the evidence sought from the CMOH is likely to be material to the Provincial Court proceeding contrary to ss. 698 and 699 of the ~~Criminal Code~~. As such, the Justice of the Peace did not have jurisdiction to issue the subpoena, and it should be quashed on this basis.

9. Mr. King explained the reason for the subpoena in the document he attached as Schedule A to the subpoena. It is clear that Mr. King seeks evidence relating to the rationale for orders issued by the CMOH under the Act: he seeks evidence about the "crafting of the statutes".

APPENDIX A-2

Published online 2020 Jul 2. doi: 10.1016/j.addr.2020.06.026

PMID: 32622021

Lipid nanoparticle technology for therapeutic gene regulation in the liver

Dominik Witzigmann,[a,b,1] Jayesh A. Kulkarni,[b,c,d,1] Jerry Leung,[a] Sam Chen,[a,e] Pieter R. Cullis,[a,b,*] and Roy van der Meel[f]

▸ Author information ▸ Article notes ▸ Copyright and License information   Disclaimer

Abstract

Go to: ☑

Hereditary genetic disorders, cancer, and infectious diseases of the liver affect millions of people around the globe and are a major public health burden. Most contemporary treatments offer limited relief as they generally aim to alleviate disease symptoms. Targeting the root cause of diseases originating in the liver by regulating malfunctioning genes with nucleic acid-based drugs holds great promise as a therapeutic approach. However, employing nucleic acid therapeutics *in vivo* is challenging due to their unfavorable characteristics. Lipid nanoparticle (LNP) delivery technology is a revolutionary development that has enabled clinical translation of gene therapies. LNPs can deliver siRNA, mRNA, DNA, or gene-editing complexes, providing opportunities to treat hepatic diseases by silencing pathogenic genes, expressing therapeutic proteins, or correcting genetic defects. Here we discuss the state-of-the-art LNP technology for hepatic gene therapy including formulation design parameters, production methods, preclinical development and clinical translation.

Keywords: Gene therapy, liver, lipid nanoparticle (LNP), lipids, hepatocyte, small interfering RNA (siRNA), messenger RNA (mRNA), DNA, guide RNA (gRNA), CRISPR/Cas9, gene silencing, gene expression, gene editing

Try out **PMC Labs** and tell us what you think. Learn More.

Elsevier Public Health Emergency Collection

Public Health Emergency COVID-19 Initiative

Adv Drug Deliv Rev. 2020; 159: 344–363.
Published online 2020 Jul 2. doi: 10.1016/j.addr.2020.06.026

PMCID: PMC7329694
PMID: 32622921

Formats:

Article | PubReader | PDF (2.1M) | Cite

Share

📘 Facebook | 📑 Twitter | 🔴 Google+

Lipid nanoparticle technology for therapeutic gene regulation in the liver

Dominik Witzigmann,[a,b,1] Jayesh A. Kulkarni,[b,c,d,1] Jerry Leung,[a] Sam Chen,[a,e] Pieter R. Cullis,[a,b,*] and Roy van der Meel[f]

▸ Author information ▸ Article notes ▸ Copyright and License information   Disclaimer

This article has been cited by other articles in PMC.

Abstract

Go to: ⊙

Hereditary genetic disorders, cancer, and infectious diseases of the liver affect millions of people around the globe and are a major public health burden. Most contemporary treatments offer limited relief as they generally aim to alleviate disease symptoms. Targeting the root cause of diseases originating in the liver by regulating malfunctioning genes with nucleic acid-based drugs holds great promise as a therapeutic approach. However, employing nucleic acid therapeutics in vivo is challenging due to their unfavorable characteristics. Lipid nanoparticle (LNP) delivery technology is a revolutionary development that has enabled clinical translation of gene therapies. LNPs can deliver siRNA, mRNA, DNA, or gene-editing complexes, providing opportunities to treat hepatic diseases by silencing pathogenic genes, expressing therapeutic proteins, or correcting genetic defects. Here we discuss the state-of-the-art LNP technology for hepatic gene therapy including formulation design parameters, production methods, preclinical development and clinical translation.

Keywords: Gene therapy, liver, lipid nanoparticle (LNP), lipids, hepatocyte, small interfering RNA (siRNA), messenger RNA (mRNA), DNA, guide RNA (gRNA), CRISPR/Cas9, gene silencing, gene expression, gene editing

Save items

☆ Add to Favorites ▾

Similar articles in PubMed

Lipid Nanoparticle Technology for Clinical Translation of siRNA Therapeutics.   [Acc Chem Res. 2019]

Lipid Nanoparticle Systems for Enabling Gene Therapies   [Mol Ther. 2017]

Lipid Nanoparticles Enabling Gene Therapies: From Concepts to Clinical Utility.   [Nucleic Acid Ther. 2018]

Ionizable lipid nanoparticles encapsulating barcoded mRNA for accelerated in vivo delivery screening   [J Control Release. 2019]

Lipid Nanoparticle Formulations for Enhanced Co-delivery of siRNA and mRNA.   [Nano Lett. 2018]

See reviews...

See all...

Cited by other articles in PMC

An Overview of the Role of Long Non-Coding RNAs in Human Choriocarcinoma   [International Journal of Molec...]

Novel vectors and approaches for gene therapy in liver diseases   [JHEP Reports. 2021]

Lipophilic Re(CO)3Pyca Complexes for Mid-IR Imaging Applications   [Dalton transactions (Cambridge...]

mRNA vaccine for cancer immunotherapy   [Molecular Cancer. 2021]

://www.ncbi.nlm.nih.gov/pmc/articles/PMC7329694/

verr / Inbox 📧 (550,342 unread) - cos... ⊕ Restore Session 📘 (2) Facebook 💬 (1) Love Unlimited Orc... 𝕸 Private - New York Cit...

indicating FIX expression can rescue hemophilia B phenotypes [²⁰⁴].

Gene editing is the next major application of mRNA therapeutics. Various approaches have been explored including CRISPR/Cas9 and zinc-finger nucleases (ZFN). An initial gene editing demonstration used a combination of viral delivery (sgRNA and repair template) combined with LNP-mRNA encoding Cas9 to correct a mutation in the fumarylacetoacetate hydrolase gene [²⁰⁵]. The study showed approximately 6% of hepatocytes were edited and it is assumed that the limitation was the viral delivery. Comparatively, Finn *et al.* used LNP-mRNA formulations encoding for Cas9 protein, co-delivered with sgRNA targeting *ttr*. They showed sustained 12-month circulating TTR knockdown (97%) following a single administration of 3 mg/kg RNA body weight in a murine model with ~70% editing in the liver (~70% liver cells are hepatocytes) [²⁰⁶]. Similarly, LNP-mediated delivery of mRNA encoding ZFN targeting *ttr* and *pcsk9* resulted in > 90% knockout at mRNA doses 10-fold lower than reported previously [¹³⁷]. In the same study, co-delivery of LNP-mRNA encoding ZFN targeting the albumin gene and a viral vector for templates of promotor-less human *IDS* or *FIX* resulted in integration of those templates at the albumin locus and generated therapeutically relevant levels of those proteins in murine models. In addition to continuous efforts in optimizing ionizable cationic lipids for enhanced genome editing in the liver, a recent study by Cheng *et al.* demonstrated that bioengineering LNP formulations with additional lipids, so-called selective organ targeting (SORT) molecules, can tune the LNP's efficiency and biodistribution. Adding 20 mol% of an ionizable cationic lipid such as DODAP significantly enhanced the genome editing in the liver, while addition of cationic or anionic SORT molecules enabled specific gene regulation in the lung or spleen [²⁰⁷,²⁰⁸].

5. Clinical translation of lipid nanotechnology

Go to: ⊙

The rapid translation from lab bench to patients was primarily driven by a holistic design of LNP composition and processes to support scalability while maintaining potency. Onpattro® paved the way for the next generation of lipid-based therapeutics and its success in phase 2 trials spurred development of mRNA therapeutics. Gene therapies enabled by LNPs are under clinical development for a broad range of applications (Table 4) [²¹¹]. In this section we discuss the clinical data for Onpattro® and some mRNA therapeutics currently under development.

Table 4

Highlighted LNP-based nucleic acid therapeutics in the clinic. Drug products in clinical development or approved by the U.S. Food and Drug Administration (FDA) and the European Medicines Agency (EMA). Company code names, generic (non-proprietary) names and company names for the products are given in brackets. Table adapted from Kulkarni *et al.* [¹⁸]

Product	Nucleic acid / transgene	Indication	Administration route	Clinical stage	Ref.
Gene silencing					

APPENDIX A-3

Drugs and Supplements   🖶 Print

Sars-Cov-2 (Covid-19) Vaccine, Adenovirus 26 Vector (Janssen) (Intramuscular Route)

Description and Brand
Names

Before Using

Proper Use

Precautions

Side Effects

Products and services

The Mayo Clinic Diet

What is your
weight-loss goal?

5-10 lbs »

11-25 lbs »

25+ lbs »

Free E-newsletter

**Subscribe to
Housecall**

Our general interest
e-newsletter keeps you
up to date on a wide
variety of health topics.

Sign up now

Side Effects

Drug information provided by: IBM Micromedex

Along with its needed effects, a medicine may cause some
unwanted effects. Although not all of these side effects may
occur, if they do occur they may need medical attention.

Check with your doctor or nurse immediately if any of the
following side effects occur:

More common

- Difficulty in moving
- fever
- headache
- joint pain or swelling
- muscle aches, cramping, pains, or stiffness
- nausea
- unusual tiredness or weakness

Incidence not known

- Anxiety
- black, tarry stools
- bleeding gums
- blood in the urine or stool
- blurred vision
- chest pain
- confusion
- continuing ringing or buzzing or other unexplained noise in
  the ears
- cough

- dizziness or lightheadedness
- fainting
- fast heartbeat
- hearing loss
- hives or welts, itching, skin rash
- inability to move the arms and legs
- numbness, weakness, or tingling in the arms or legs
- pain, redness, or swelling in the arm or leg
- pinpoint red spots on the skin
- redness of the skin
- seizures
- stomach pain
- trouble breathing
- unusual bleeding or bruising
- vomiting blood

Some side effects may occur that usually do not need medical attention. These side effects may go away during treatment as your body adjusts to the medicine. Also, your health care professional may be able to tell you about ways to prevent or reduce some of these side effects. Check with your health care professional if any of the following side effects continue or are bothersome or if you have any questions about them:

More common

- Pain, redness, or swelling at the injection site

Other side effects not listed may also occur in some patients. If you notice any other effects, check with your healthcare professional.

Call your doctor for medical advice about side effects. You may report side effects to the FDA at 1-800-FDA-1088.

Appendix A-4

https://www.ncbi.nlm.nih.gov/pmc/articles/PMC7329694/

Fiverr / Inbox   (550,342 unread) - cos...   Restore Session   (2) Facebook   (1) Love Unlimited Orc...   Private - New York Cit...

4. Preclinical development and rationale for lipid nanotechnology   Go to: ⊙

Research in the late 1980s focusing on *in vivo* pDNA delivery showed that in the absence of a delivery system, naked nucleic acid injected into the circulation rapidly broke down and the products accumulated in hepatic tissue [166]. As interest towards ASOs and siRNA grew, LNP compositions and production methods simply translated from plasmids to these shorter nucleic acids [167]. More recently, formulations have become sufficiently potent to support discovery and translation of mRNA therapeutics [168]. Fig. 4 illustrates the different LNP-based treatments for hepatic diseases by silencing pathogenic genes, expressing therapeutic proteins, or correcting genetic defects. Table 3 highlights preclinical LNP-based hepatic gene therapy approaches.

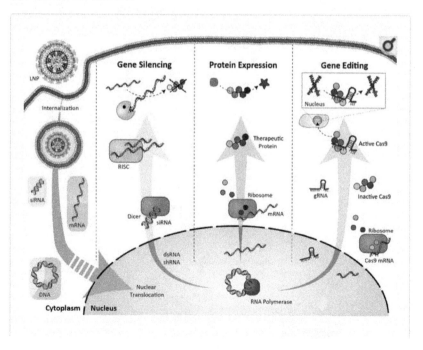

○ 🔒 https://www.britannica.com/science/messenger-RNA

kela - G... ⓘ Fiverr / Inbox ✉ (550,342 unread) - cos... ⊕ Restore Session ⓕ (2) Facebook ▣ (1) Love Unlimited Orc... 𝓜 Private - New York Cit... M Sample photos - agor... ▯

🔍 Search   Quizzes   Games   On This Day

transcription). Each molecule of mRNA encodes the information for one protein (or more than one protein in bacteria), with each sequence of three nitrogen-containing bases in the mRNA specifying the incorporation of a particular amino acid within the protein. The mRNA molecules are transported through the nuclear envelope into the cytoplasm, where they are translated by the rRNA of ribosomes (*see* translation).

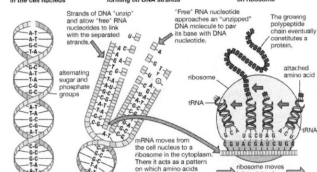

protein synthesis

DNA in the cell nucleus carries a genetic code, which consists of sequences of adenine (A), thymine (T), guanine (G), and cytosine (C) (Figure 1). RNA, which contains uracil (U) instead of thymine, carries the code to protein-making sites in the cell. To make RNA, DNA pairs its bases with those of the "free" nucleotides (Figure 2). Messenger RNA (mRNA) then travels to the ribosomes in the cell cytoplasm, where protein synthesis occurs (Figure 3). The base triplets of transfer RNA (tRNA) pair with those of mRNA and at the same time deposit their amino acids on the growing protein chain. Finally, the synthesized protein is released to perform its task in the cell or elsewhere in the body.

Image: Encyclopædia Britannica, Inc.

APPENDIX A-5

REVIEW article
Front. Neurosci., 16 November 2018 | https://doi.org/10.3389/fnins.2018.00843

A New Frontier: The Convergence of Nanotechnology, Brain Machine Interfaces, and Artificial Intelligence

Gabriel A. Silva*

Departments of Bioengineering and Neurosciences, Center for Engineered Natural Intelligence, University of California San Diego, La Jolla, CA, United States

A confluence of technological capabilities is creating an opportunity for machine learning and artificial intelligence (AI) to enable "smart" nanoengineered brain machine interfaces (BMI). This new generation of technologies will be able to communicate with the brain in ways that support contextual learning and adaptation to changing functional requirements. This applies to both invasive technologies aimed at restoring neurological function, as in the case of neural prosthesis, as well as non-invasive technologies enabled by signals such as electroencephalograph (EEG). Advances in computation, hardware, and algorithms that learn and adapt in a contextually dependent way will be able to leverage the capabilities that nanoengineering offers the design and functionality of BMI. We explore the enabling capabilities that these devices may exhibit, why they matter, and the state of the technologies necessary to build them. We also discuss a number of open technical challenges and problems that will need to be solved in order to achieve this.

APPENDIX 1

Dr. Christiane Northrup Discusses the COVID-19 Vaccine

Excerpts of video interview with Polly Tommey, Executive Director of *PeepsTV*

YouTube. Posted October 7, 2020.
https://www.youtube.com/watch?v=UcGZC9P9WBg

[1:59] Christiane: Yes, there has never been a vaccine like this. It's an RNA vaccine, it is what's called a trans-infection. It will fundamentally change people's DNA, and what I don't like about it, even more than the usual thing about the toxic metals that are in vaccines, that make our bodies literally into an antenna, with 5G, this one has the usual non-human DNA like, you know, monkeys, maybe fetal cells, pigs, whatever. And so, it begins to make us, what's called chimers, C-H-I-M-E-R, introducing non-human DNA into our bodies. What is worse though, is that there is a patent and work that they've done at MIT, to make a dye, and the patent of the dye is called "luciferase". And under a light you'd be able to see who was vaccinated, who wasn't, and the deal is to store your biometric information, because this vaccine will have nanoparticles, nanocrystalline particles that are inten... actually little robots, like little antennas. And they will have the ability to take your biometric data, not only your vaccine record, but your breathing, your heart rate, your activities, sexual activities, drugs that you're taking, where you travel, all of that and then take that data and store it in the cloud. What's even more concerning, is that the Bill and Melinda Gates Foundation, on March 26, 2020, applied for a patent, patent number 060606, to take that biometric data, give you a barcode and connect each of us to cryptocurrency so that we would become, literally, slaves to the system. Like, everything pri... it would be the end of privacy, the end of freedom, because who gets the data? Who uses the data and what do they do with it? So, this... this patent to connect the vaccinated to crypto-currency, making all humans a commodity, is extremely concerning. And everyone should be concerned, given that this is a virus from which 99.9% of people recover. So, I would ask why do we need anything like this? Because it goes far beyond those pandemics of old, small pox and so on, this is very different. The plan here is to vaccinate the entire world and the narrative that we're being sold is, things will not go back to normal until everyone is vaccinated. Vaccinated with what? A transfection thing that we've never seen before? And by the way, once those nanoparticles go in, there's no detoxing from them, there's no getting them out of there. They combine with your DNA and you're suddenly programmable and with the proposed 5G networks, the body would be an antenna, where you could be controlled from outside of yourself. That's kind of worst-case scenario. That's what bothers me about the vaccine, and so far, in the initial Moderna trials, 100% of the people who got the high-dose vaccine, and remember, these were very, very healthy people, very healthy, the kind that there are very few of. Since we now have a planet, and at least in the United States, where 54% of all children have a chronic disease. So, 100% of those people had side effects, severe side effects. And in the lower dose, 80% of people had side effects. And as my colleague, Bruce Lipton says, these are not side-effects, these are effects. And some of them have been this thing called "transverse myelitis", which is, essentially, polio. And so, those are, those are my concerns about everyone lining up to get this vaccine and that has also been fast-tracked. There will be, or have not been, animal studies in the past, when they have tried to do this kind of vaccine in animals, the animals appeared to be fine, initially, and then, after a while when their bodies came into contact with the germ they were vaccinated for, they had what's called pathogenic priming, that somehow, the vaccine did something to the immune system so that they got very sick later, when they were actually introduced to the pathogen. So, we don't know whether or not that would happen.

[06:54] Polly: So, a few questions coming in on this vaccine, if we can just break it down a little for the average person like myself, who maybe doesn't even know what a nanoparticle... I do, but say some people don't even know what a nanoparticle is. But the other question coming in, is that the press and the other side is saying oh, don't listen to these doctors and these nonsense people, these quacks that say there's nanoparticles, there's hydrogel, there's luciferase in that, it's nonsense. So, they're barefaced lying to the public.

[07:24] Christiane: Yes, they are. And if you'd like, I could send you the papers from MIT where they're talking about this, you know, so that you have the references. It's fascinating that in my opinion now, as a holistic physician for years, everything that I always thought was a good idea like IV vitamin C, has been demonized. You cannot patent a naturally occurring substance. And so, for my entire career, many of the things that I thought were a really good idea and that I saw were very highly accepted, various herbs, homeopathic medicine, this sort of thing, that was very actively downplayed. And a lot of that is from, in 1920, the Flexner Report of John D. Rockefeller, where he invented the word "quack" and went after all the naturopathic medical schools, the homeopathic medical schools and so on. So, there's been very active and unpurposed vilification of natural medicine, and the human's ability to be healthy. I think this is the thing, that what we're really looking at is a paradigm shift from the germ theory of disease, you are sick because of germs, to the terrain theory. Let me put that very simply; All right, the germ theory is, you have a fish tank, the water's dirty, vaccinate the fish. That's the germ theory. The terrain theory is, clean the water, and the fish will remain healthy. There you have it.

. . . .

[10:36] Polly: So, they're pushing the flu vaccine, and a lot of people are taking it, because the media is saying we've got to keep the hospitals free, you've got to do your bit as a British person or as an American, you've got to help out. So, the people are flocking, there's lines in Britain of people lining up for the flu vaccine to do their bit for Britain. And then, so, that's one thing, but I really want to get across to everybody, and you described this so well, and I'm sorry to make you, but could you just do it one more time? This COVID vaccine is like nothing we've seen before. Am I correct in that?

[11:07] Christiane: That is correct. Nothing, we have no experience with this at all. A nanoparticle is a tiny, tiny, tiny robot, that collects your biometric data, your heart rate, your breathing, your relationships, whether you've had sex, what drugs you're on, where you're going, who are you going with, and sends that data up to the cloud. And then they want to use that data to, at the very best, you know, sell you stuff. Like, know your every move so that they can send you emails to get whatever product, but at the very worst, this one about connecting you to cryptocurrency, so that we have a cashless society, facial recognition, the ability to control a whole population and, and there are aspects of this that are very nefarious which is that, with 5G then rolled out, which is being rolled out in some places, that 60GHz, and that vibration, that radiation can literally adversely affect the haemoglobin in our bodies, making it very hard to be oxygenated. And that looked like what was happening, by the way, in China at the beginning and also New York City, where people would come in, unable to, you know, blue, unable to get enough oxygen. And then they were put on respirators and killed that way, because that wasn't what was necessary.

[12:42] Polly: This "luciferase", what is, why would they call it that?

[12:49] Christiane: Well, because Lucifer means light, and, but you know, but we could get into the Luciferian agenda, but I would rather not. It's very scary and it's very dark and this is probably not the place for it, but if you, if you wanted to get into that, there are certainly resources available. I'm not real happy about the Bill and Melinda Gates patent as 060606, in the Book of Revelation this is the Mark of the Beast. And according to those who have studied this kind of thing, there are many symbols that are associated with this agenda, including masking everyone so that we can't see each other's faces and then, in the U.K. now, no more than six people can get together at the same time. Why six people, six feet, a patent six, six, six... I think that there is something else going on, other than public health, that's what I would say. And having, having testified at the vaccine mandate hearings in our state, I can tell you that, one after another, parents went and testified about their vaccine injured child and what had happened when they went in for the routine vaccinations. And, almost to a person, the doctors in my profession, acted as though this was not happening, that they, they would pare it back, all vaccines are safe and effective, side effects are one in a million. And my career is based on the fact that I actually listened to what my patients told me, because we have the ability to know. You, as a mother, you have the ability to know, I know that this is what did that to my child. As, as my colleague, Andy Wakefield, says, maternal intuition is the whole reason that the human race has survived as long as it has. And I think we need to listen to that maternal intuition. Right now, for instance, my, my profession is vaccinating healthy, pregnant women against flu and DTaP. I don't understand it. Then we are vaccinating 99% of all our infants with hepatitis B vaccine, which contains 15 times more aluminium than is recommended by the FDA. So that we now have an entire generation of infants who have been injected with the toxic heavy metals and the poisons that are in vaccines, at a time when their brain isn't even fully developed yet. I don't understand it and I don't see how you can do it.

And quite frankly I'd like to, you know, say I believe this is a crime against humanity.

[15:48] Polly: So, you're talking about a mother's gut instinct, and we had that when we took our children in to be vaccinated, and then of course the doctors or the media, all of the things that are still going today, puts the fear into you and then you override your gut instinct, which is happening right now with the COVID, we've seen it already. And so, I, I really do feel that fear, fear is the biggest evil of, of all here, because we're all living by it. You, you're a doctor, you're sitting here, you're telling the truth. Why are your colleagues not doing it? There are a handful of doctors around the world and of course the German doctor arrested in Great Britain this weekend for just standing on the podium, didn't even get to speak. So, is that fear again in the doctors, or is…

. . . .

[21:35] Christiane: The first thing we all need to do, is we need to reach out to each other and form "pods", freedom pods all over the planet. There are very few of them. Let's remember, this is an agenda put forward by very, very few people, and if we all stand up and say, we're not having it, and I would start now. One of the things that we're noticing in the United

States, is the number of people who are now home schooling their children, as a result of the vaccine mandates in the State of Maine, in the State of New York and so on. So, we're finding women, in particular, creating these sisterhoods where we are educating our own children. Let us remove ourselves from these top-down authoritarian people who tell you, you need them to live. As we begin to move, at this time, through what I am calling the great awakening where enormous amounts of light… This has been prophesied, by the way, by many seers for centuries. This is the time now, the great awakening, but we must bond together. And so, for instance, I've become a single-issue voter, every single politician I, that I am going to vote for, I ask them one question: 'How do you feel about mandated vaccines?' If their answer is, 'I'm not sure', then I go, 'Next!' I want someone who is going to say to me, 'I stand for sovereignty and medical freedom.' Then I will vote for them. And we're finding that there are movements all over the planet. Dr. Pam Popper, Peggy Hall, people all over the planet, the New Earth Society, Sacha Stone, many, many people all rising together. If there's anything that is going to bring us all together, it is this. And I listened to Kevin Jenkins of the Newark Urban Health League, and he said, 'As a black man, I understand slavery. This vaccine is a gateway to enslave all of humanity.' And what they're doing in Newark is, they're standing up to the narrative of black people are, black people are vulnerable to COVID, let's vaccinate the black people first. And in Newark, what they're doing is holding a rally every Monday, and the politicians are now saying, please stop that, because what they're saying to the politicians, to the public health officials, 'You take the vaccine first, we will watch you for a year, then we'll consider it, because we, as black people, remember the Tuskegee Experiment, we remember what has been done to us in the name of public health, you go first.' Now, if enough of us did that, then we would find that it would all end. And that's why I'm standing up at this, at this particular time. I feel like I was born for this, my whole career has led me up to this.

Appendix 2

Biometric Tattoos: Pfizer and the coming Brave New World?

The introduction of a biometric 'tattoo' has been one of the talking points with the development of a coronavirus vaccine. For some, developing a vaccine that uses biometric technology is meant to act as a form of population control and can be linked directly or indirectly to a future world order.

According to Worldometer[1], there have been over 53 million coronavirus cases worldwide leading to over 1.3 million deaths. As many nations begin to slowly get over the effect of the virus, pharmaceutical companies and health agencies globally are working to develop an effective vaccine against the novel coronavirus.

Pfizer, an American pharmaceutical company, has begun production of a vaccine at its Belgium branch in the municipality of Puurs in Antwerp. The company is partnering with BioNtech, a German technological company, to supply over 1.2 billion doses of the COVID-19 vaccine[2] next year.

In a joint announcement, Pfizer and BioNtech announced early this November that the vaccine they have developed is "90% effective" against COVID-19 after the first initial analysis of their phase 3 clinical trial–which is the final stage before an application for approval.

While the vaccine is still awaiting approval from health authorities, it is already being produced at the two Pfizer locations – at their Puurs site in Belgium and their Michigan site in the U.S.

"We have already produced hundreds of thousands of doses at both sites," said Koen Colpaert of Pfizer in Belgium in a report.

However, there are several controversial and talking points of the coronavirus vaccination, one of which is the introduction of biometric identification.

An announcement[3] was made early July 2020 of a private-public partnership between financial platform giants, Mastercard, AI identity authentication company, Trust Stamp, and GAVI (officially Gavi, the Vaccine Alliance) – a company heavily backed by billionaire philanthropist Bill Gates.

Testing is scheduled to begin soon in "low-income, remote communities" in West Africa for the biometric ID which will also double as a payment system and vaccination record. The biometric digital identity platform that "evolves just as you evolve" was first announced in late 2018 and will integrate Trust Stamp's digital identity platform into the GAVI-Mastercard "Wellness Pass," a digital vaccination record and identity system that is also linked to Mastercard's click-to-play system that is powered by its AI and machine learning technology called NuData.

What then is the implication of having these "biometric tattoos" imprinted on everyone? For starters, the continuous preference for vaccine trials in Africa has become a sensitive and controversial issue, due to several instances of Western researchers conducting unethical trials in African countries.[4] Many foreign scientists have been accused of undertaking medical experiments on people of African origin even in the U.S.

Early this year, a group of French scientists were heavily criticized for suggesting that Africa is a suitable location for testing vaccines against COVID-19 because "there are no masks, no treatments, no resuscitation". This statement was heavily condemned by Dr. Tedros Adhanom Ghebreyesus, Director-General of the World Health Organization.

However, instances like this have created a cloud of uncertainty over the ethical engagement of those involved in coronavirus vaccine trials across Africa.

The incorporation of this biometric digital identity platform with the coronavirus vaccination process has increased speculation over a New World Order.[5]

While some are poking fun at these conspiracy theories, others are well in support of the views that the coronavirus outbreak is an intentional effort to push an unknown agenda led by big pharmaceutical companies like Pfizer and leveraging on technology – especially with Bill Gates, Mastercard and Trust Stamp now in the mix.

Vaccination against the coronavirus would be voluntary, however, with Mastercard's soon to be launched Wellness Pass program involving GAVI and Trust Stamp, there are some concerns. The Wellness program would be launched first in West Africa alongside a COVID-19 vaccination program when an approved vaccine becomes available.

But many are pointing to the fact that while this biometric implant vaccination would be voluntary, there is a caveat to it that may reveal other unethical plans.

The biometric ID system, which is heavily backed by Mastercard, utilizes a technology called Evergreen Hash that creates an AI-generated "3D mask" based on a single image of a person's fingerprint, face or palm. According to Gareth Genner, CEO of

Trust Stamp, the original data containing an individual's name or other traditional identifiers is replaced with encryption keys once the 3D mask is created.

However, a huge cause for concern with the new Wellness Pass program is its connection to digital cashless payment solutions–which has been the core of MasterCard's business model. This could mean that this digital ID would soon become mandatory especially since cashless and touchless methods of payment have always been seen as a mode of transmitting infection by GAVI and regulatory bodies like the World Health Organization since the pandemic began early this year.

Subsequently, without this new biometric ID, people may not be able to access certain essential services such as healthcare, food, and transportation amongst other things.

Some Christian groups are kicking against this mode of vaccination[6] saying that it constitutes accepting the "Mark of the Beast" spoken of in the Bible. While other groups are saying that the technology has nothing to do with the anti-Christ and just needs to be understood better.

Whatever the case may be, there is the overall feeling that the entire pandemic and vaccination programs were premeditated considering the urgency shown in developing and testing a vaccine.

According to Céline Deluzarche, in an article on *Futura-Sciences*,[7] "it takes between 15 and 20 years to obtain an effective, non-toxic and usable vaccine" due to the several steps and studies involved in creating a safe vaccine for large scale use.

With Pfizer, Mastercard and GAVI working on a biometric ID vaccination program, there is the theory that it is going to be used for population control and surveillance by the ruling class.

Billionaire Bill Gates, whose foundation has contributed millions to the research and development of a coronavirus vaccine, has already come out to debunk these theories[8] of using digital implants to control the population.

While there is still no FDA-approved drug or vaccine for the coronavirus, questions are still continually being asked by members of the public concerning the safety of these vaccines in production.

References

1. Coronavirus Cases. (2020). *Worldometer*. Accessed November 14, 2020. *https://www.worldometers.info/coronavirus/*

2. Pfizer's Belgian site will produce millions of doses of COVID-19 vaccine. (November 9, 2020). *The Brussels Times*. Accessed November 14, 2020. *https://www.brusselstimes.com/news/ belgium-all-news/140059/pfizers-belgian-site-will-produce-millions-of-doses-of-covid-19-vaccine-puurs-antwerp-biontech-kalamazoo-michigan-koen-colpaert/*

3. Public-private partnership launches biometrics identity and vaccination record system in West Africa. (July 10, 2020). Privacy International. Accessed November 14, 2020. *https:// privacyinternational.org/examples/4083/public-private-partnership-launches-biometrics-identity-and-vaccination-record-system*

4. First African trial of a COVID-19 vaccine. (June 30, 2020). GAVI. Accessed November 15, 2020. *https://www.gavi.org/ vaccineswork/first-african-trial-covid-19-vaccine*

5. Miracle cures, New World Order and a Bill Gates plan: The most absurd Coronavirus conspiracy theories. (October 6, 2020). *Moneycontrol*. Accessed November 15, 2020. *https://*

*www.moneycontrol.com/news/photos/coronavirus/miracle-
cures-new-world-order-and-a-bill-gates-plan-the-most-absurd-
coronavirus-conspiracy-theories-5930401.html*

6. Biometrics, Fingerprint Technology, and the Mark of the
   Beast. (August 22, 2012). Calvary Chapel Jonesboro. Accessed
   November 14, 2020. *https://www.calvarychapeljonesboro.
   org/prophecynews/biometrics-fingerprint-technology-
   and-the-mark-of-the-beast*

7. The COVID-19 Vaccine. The Imposition of Compulsory
   Vaccination with a Biometric Health Passport? (October 3,
   2020). *SGT Report.* Accessed November 15, 2020. *https://www.
   sgtreport.com/2020/10/the-covid-19-vaccine-the-imposition-
   of-compulsory-vaccination-with-a-biometric-health-passport/*

8. Bill Gates denies conspiracy theories that say he wants to use
   coronavirus vaccines to implant tracking devices. (July 22,
   2020). *CNBC News.* Accessed November 15, 2020. *https://
   www.cnbc.com/2020/07/22/bill-gates-denies-conspiracy-theor-
   ies-that-say-he-wants-to-use-coronavirus-vaccines-to-implant-
   tracking-devices.html*